Please Abuse Me... Said No One

*Searching for Love
while Overcoming
the Secrets and Pain
of My Past*

WYETHA E. COX

Cover design, editing, formatting, and layout by University of Moguls Publishing and Design
www.universityofmoguls.com

ISBN-13:

For speaking engagements and bulk book orders:
Wyetha Cox
www.wyethaecox.com

Instagram:
@Wysunique

Facebook:
Wyetha Cox

Dedication

To my mother who was the rock that set my foundation, who was a living testimony of a strong black woman who didn't have much but always did the right things to provide for her children and kept her dignity to the end even during her illness... she kept her head up with the grace of God on her side! I am so thankful every day for the strength that she imparted to me and showed me that the situation may look impossible, but God can turn it around.

To my Uncle Michael and my Aunt Tootie, who have passed before I could share this moment, they were a wonderful example of a proud couple, they provided for not just their own family but who also looked out for me and my children. I knew that when my son needed a positive male role model and a stern talk, all I had to do was call on my uncle anytime. My aunt was a sweet person who I needed as a mother figure and even though she had her medical struggles, she was a blessing during the time I needed it.

To my godmother and my mother's best friend, thank you for being there through all the ups and downs, always ready with prayers to encourage me to push through to my blessings.

Acknowledgements

To my daughters Miya and Nicole, I love you and am proud to see all the progress in your lives. My prayer for the both of you is that you carry with you all the positive images I have shown you and hope that you don't repeat my mistakes. Always remember you can be strong and persevere through anything with God as your base.

To my son, Emmanuel, who I am so proud of. For your strength while you served in the military during some perilous times… you prevailed and you have showed yourself to be a good person even though you didn't have your biological father around. You have shown that having a positive upbringing can produce a good man, and it's only a confirmation when you married your best friend Janelle.

To my spiritual friend, sister in Christ, and supporter, Mercedes, I love you for your realness and your knack of never sugar-coating the truth whenever I came to you with whatever I was going through. You have been there whether it was a mountain top or valley experience or even if I just needed to talk or share a praise report. I always knew your ear was available, so for that, I thank God for you.

To my sister from another mother, Robin, who I could call to talk, vent or be my social media detective any time, thanks for being there during the tough times while we worked at Bowie State. Who would have ever guessed we would become good friends and our families would get along so well?

To my friend Christa, who had to be appointed as my guardian angel sent to protect my mental peace while housed at the shelter... who was there for me so many times I can't keep track and even though our backgrounds and life stories were different in many ways, we came to a crossroads at The Lighthouse, the friendship bond we developed there would transcend beyond the walls of the shelter and I thank God for meeting you. I pray I can be a better friend to you than you have been to me.

To Lolita Walker, a woman who renewed and allowed me to unmask my inner me so that I could remember what had been spoken over my life as my purpose! If I hadn't attended her retreat, this book may have not been published due to so many distractions and stumbling blocks that I allowed to cloud my focus. But God had a plan and He used her, and for that, I am grateful.

Introduction

This book had to be written, but only when the timing of God's plan was right. There were so many times I would start to write with good intentions of finishing and eventually publishing, but then life would get in the way—or so that is the excuse I would tell myself. Eventually, I simply stopped telling people that I was writing because I had lost the zeal to tell my story since I had stopped believing in my purpose.

My mother once said to me when I was a young girl, "God has great plans for you," and I got all excited and I said, "He does" then she said, "Yes He does, but you will have to go through some hardships to get what He has for you." So, then I quickly replied, "In that case, no thanks I don't want it then." I had no idea that that conversation would resonate so deeply in my mind and my spirit every time I went through a valley experience.

I can remember a time in my life when I was in a very bad living situation that I needed to get out of, and I found an agency to help me financially move, but at the last minute there were some complications with my job status and the agency held the funds so my move-in date had been delayed. Thank God for my friend Cynthia Leslie and her husband. With some prayer and persistence, I was able to move in. So, when they gave me the key and I stepped inside my apartment, I gave God some true praise, and laid prostrate on the floor in prayer. At that moment, God revealed my mission in a vision of me standing in front of a large group of women sharing my story.

As time progressed, God would send many people in my life to confirm that I needed to continue to write my story. However, when I ended up living in a shelter, I felt like a failure. I asked myself, "How can I help others in the state that I'm in?" and I had mentally given up hope of finishing my book, and then I met a woman of God named Cynthia Rawles while I was in the shelter. She gifted me her book, titled, "Live in Your Purpose… Don't Throw in the Towel." The words in her book would re-ignite my passion to finish my story. However, it would take another couple of years to officially set a date to launch my book due to some discouraging obstacles that I allowed into my life. That silenced my passion to write and again, God sent a messenger to allow me to drop the spirit of procrastination for good. I attended a Women's Weekend Renewal Retreat in February 2019 that allowed me to put in writing and declare on my vision board that I would become a published author by December 31st of 2020!

This book is based on my true story. Some characters' names have been changed and characters have been merged to protect the innocent and the guilty.

Table of Contents

Chapter 1   Strong Foundation 1

Chapter 2   Childhood Trauma 4

Chapter 3   Identity Crisis 12

Chapter 4   New Mother Decisions 23

Chapter 5   Mom's Last Goodbye 34

Chapter 6   Vulnerable Life Lessons 45

Chapter 7   Losing Control 58

Chapter 8   Family Betrayal 73

Chapter 9   African Chameleon 89

Chapter 10   Vagabond Blues 101

Chapter 11   Diamond in the Rough 114

Strong Foundation

My earliest memories were of many visits to Children's National Hospital and I can still see the colorful design on the floors. It was four colors and each color represented a different part of the hospital to tell you where to go depending on your destination. I can remember seeing many different doctors. Some I did see more than once even though I cannot remember how long I was seen there… but I do remember a thick folder that was my chart. I believe I asked my mother about a scar I had noticed on my stomach and she mentioned that I had surgery when I was incredibly young. I have a few vague flashes of memories of my mother and me taking buses to travel to the hospital.

I have glimpses of memories when there were times that my mom, my sister, and I spent time together but there were also many times my mother wasn't around because she was working so she could make a living to provide for us since my father wasn't around. I have never been able to get an answer to why my father was not around at the beginning of my early years. When my mom was home, she was continually active in her church and she would also spend time praying and counseling people about their walk with Christ. It was noticeably clear to me watching my mom that she projected such a positive role model of what a hard-working mother would do to take care of her children.

We had been close to a family who had lived in our building and most of the time when my mom was working, my sister and I would stay with them and they were like our extended family. This family also attended the same church as we did. That made our bond stronger and their daughter—the youngest of four siblings—became my best friend. Our mothers would dress us alike sometimes and at Christmas, we would get many similar toys. There was another neighbor that lived downstairs from us who would watch me sometimes and he was an elderly man who would watch his grandson too. The one memory about him that stuck out was he used to feed us raw hot dogs for a snack.

Later, my mother would enroll in some college classes which required more time away from home so my mom decided to hire someone to come to our house to watch and feed us. But as I remember it, the main things Ms. Cathy was good at were talking on the phone and propping her feet up while eating. I also remember her feeding us some old stale biscuits amongst other negative memories, and eventually, after telling my mom about things I had seen her do, my mom ended up firing her. I witnessed my mom do everything she could possibly do to take care and provide for us. She was the perfect example of a strong Black woman who did whatever she had to legally put her children first and never gave us up even though times got hard. Sadly, all that hard work, stress, and sacrifice took a toll on her physically and she ended up going to the doctors where she was diagnosed as having diabetes. It was explained to my mother that she needed to limit the stress in her life. That was easier said than done. She tried but it was especially hard since she had a mission and unfortunately by the time she was diagnosed, the damage to her body had already begun. Also, at that time, there was little help in medications to reverse the effects. Only to help live with it.

To understand my mother's determined attitude, you would have to look back at her upbringing. My grandfather was an immigrant from Santo Domingo, Dominican Republic who was adopted by a family once he came to the United States and later in his life, he would serve in the U.S. Military. He married my grandmother Sarah Jane Richardson and they had five children. The stories that I heard from my mom and some of her brothers was that my grandfather was a very harsh disciplinarian who ran his household as is if they were in the military—even down to the dishing out discipline. They were made to line up to receive their punishments. So it was to no surprise when my mom talked about how unbearable it was living in the same house. My mother began to look for a way out and she found it in my father. By rushing to get married, she had gotten out of her miserable situation. Unfortunately, in my mom's rush to find a way out, she did not take the time to really find out who my dad really was and that backfired on her later. She would find out he lied about his age, he misled her to believe that he was an ordained minister, he really didn't have any backbone when it came to making crucial decisions, and he really didn't like working hard. Once the truth began to come out, my mother was faced with a decision on what was she going to do and she decided to take a break from being with my father. I guess that is why I have no memories of him living with us in my early years.

I do have several regrets when it comes to my mother. One is that she sacrificed her health to provide for my sister and me. The second thing is that I didn't hear my mom telling me she loved me, nor did she show affection by hugging me even though she showed me love through her sacrifices. I also believe she did not know how to express something to us because it was never shown to her.

Chapter 2

Childhood Trauma

"Twenty-two percent of adults—female and male—
report being sexually abused as a child."
A Healing Guide for Survivors of Physical,
Sexual and Emotional Abuse

*(Adverse Childhood Experience Study, 1998. A Healing
Guide for Survivors of Physical, Sexual, and Emotional
Abuse - published in a pamphlet from the Maryland
Health Care Coalition Against Domestic Violence)*

My mother told me she must go pray for someone and I must tag along. We drove to a hotel and when we entered the room I am introduced to an interracial couple (the husband is white, and the wife is black). My mother began to speak and counsel the couple and before she could pray with them, all hell broke loose and the husband started yelling and hollering and throwing things in the room. My mom asked the couple to step outside into the hallway to try to calm the situation down but when that didn't seem to make things any better, my mom made a decision to leave. Later, my mom received a call from the wife to let my mom know that due to her husband's outburst and damage to the room, the hotel management requested that they leave which caused her to break down in tears because she said that they didn't have anywhere else to go!

When my mom told me about what happened I thought how sad that they would end up homeless so I thought about it and suggested to my mom that we should invite them to come stay with us until they could find another place to stay. Several days later, the couple ended up coming to stay with us. The day that would change my life forever happened about a week later. My uncle was going to play on a non-professional baseball team that evening so the husband that was staying with us named Donald asked if he could use another person to play on the team so my uncle told him he was welcome to come and play. When we were all leaving to go to the game, we saw my mother walking up the street and we stopped to ask her if she wanted to go to the game with us. She said that she was going to take care of something later and then she asked my aunt if she could take my sister and me over to her house after the game. My aunt agreed.

During the baseball game, my little sister had an accident on herself and Donald hurt his hand during the game so we had to leave the game early. While we were on our way home, Donald told my aunt that he would watch my sister and me until my mother got home so she didn't have to worry about watching us and we would already be home when my mother got back. My aunt agreed and dropped Donald, my sister, and me off at our house.

My aunt left us in the care of a stranger so she would not be bothered with taking care of us and therefore, I had a hard time forgiving her! Once in the house, I took off my sister's soiled clothes and washed her up and put her pajamas on her and put her to bed. Then I proceeded to put my night clothes on. Before I got into bed, Donald asked me to come inside the room where he and his wife had been staying in and when I entered, that's when I noticed that his wife wasn't home. He asked me if I wanted to lay on the bed and watch some TV and I said yes! One of many decisions I would later regret and blame myself for repeatedly in my mind!

The next thing I knew, Donald was lying next to me on the bed and he asked me if I wanted to play a game and I said yes. He then told me that I would have to lick his penis and put it in my mouth, and I looked at him strange because I did not understand what he was asking me to do. When I looked down, he was pulling out this big fleshly organ-looking thing out of his pajama pants and I really didn't know what I was looking at then he proceeded to push my head down toward it. My tongue touched it and I could smell piss and I thought to myself that it tasted nasty. There was some hair on it and it kept getting in my mouth so I went to pull my head up and he started pushing my head back down. This happened several times and I almost gagged on it and then finally he let my head go so I could come up for air.

I was thinking it was over until he told me there was a second part to the game. For this part, I had to take my panties off so that he could examine me like a doctor. Once I took off my panties, he moved closer to me and tried to put his fleshly hairy thing inside of me. It was hurting really bad and I cried out and he said the pain would stop in a little while and he just kept trying to push it up inside my private place and I kept saying it was hurting really bad.

In my mind, I remembered hearing his wife crying one night when I walked by their room and I said to myself this is probably why she was crying because of this awful game we were playing. Finally, he stopped and told me to put my panties on and come out to the kitchen. I put on my panties and walked in the kitchen. He asked me if I was hungry and I said not really. He asked me if I had anything to eat and I said no, so he fixed me something to eat and gave it to me and I kept trying to eat but I kept feeling like I was going to throw up!

Donald then said to me: "If you even think about telling anybody about the game we played tonight, I will come after you with my false teeth." Then he took them out and showed them to me. After he took them out of his mouth, he put them in front of me and I have never seen anything like them before and they scared me! All I could think about was as soon as my mom gets home, I have got to tell her how Donald made me hurt down there! I don't know how long I sat there waiting there with this man sitting next to me but it seemed like forever even though he got up to get dressed so he can to go to the emergency room to get his wrist that he hurt at the game earlier in the evening checked out.

When my mom walked through the door, Donald left out to go to the hospital in the same cab my mom pulled up in. I was now laying on the sofa holding my stomach and my mom asked me what was wrong. I took a deep breath and I began to tell her about what had happened over the course of the evening. She put her arms around me and said, "He hurt my baby!" My mom's first call was to the police and the police arrived at the house to question me. This is where everything from this point on becomes a little fuzzy… but what I do remember is after my mother called the police, they had many questions for me from lots of male police officers where I had to repeatedly tell what happened—over and over again. The police confronted Donald with my allegations of molestation at the hospital.

His wife arrived at the hospital too and even though she stood by his side, I saw something in her eyes. I felt it was fear or maybe deep down, she knew that what I was accusing him of was really true! Donald denied everything and my mom was on the warpath. Over the next couple of months, I had to relive that terrible night repeatedly by telling my story to so many people. It was a tough time for me.

You must understand that at the time when this happened, the police force was predominately staffed by men. That made it very uncomfortable for me—to talk to a man about what another man had done to me. They wanted me to be very specific about some of the details and they also wanted me to demonstrate with my hands how far he had penetrated me! One day I had to tell my story to a group of people which I later found out was a grand jury and a woman laughed at me as I told what happened to me. It totally crushed me inside!

During that time, there were not many child psychologists or therapists to talk to, so I had all these emotions inside me and my head was spinning. Actually, I was like a zombie stuck in a little's girl's body just going through the motions and going wherever my mom, the lawyers, and the police instructed us to go. I was glad when I was finally getting a break after the grand jury proceedings.

Then the most pivotal day of my young life happened. It was the day of the trial. After many months of sharing my story, I was once again asked to go into the courtroom before a judge on a witness stand—facing lawyers, church members, and family members to tell my humiliating story all over again! I was given a cross to hold onto while I sat on the witness stand telling my story and answering the lawyer's questions.

I remember looking out into the courtroom and seeing one of the pastors from my church. It made me feel good to see a familiar face. As a young child, it was so easy for me to believe and trust that these adults knew what was best for me and that all these days of talking about my awful experience was going to be rewarded with justice! I can't remember all the questions I was asked but I do remember at one point while I was on the witness stand testifying, I squeezed the cross in my hand so hard that it made an imprint in my hand! It was very nerve-wracking, intimidating, and almost terrifying at times to see lots of lawyers.

When I had to face him staring me down while I was on the stand, I never imagined that in the end, the judge and jury would find him not guilty and he would get off! It was the first time since this whole ordeal had happened that I begin to feel real emotions come out of myself. I began to feel so many emotions at the same time. Fear, anger, hurt, and pain. I could not understand and neither did any of my other family members. I really cannot remember anything else that happened that day except that the judge had commented to my mother that he had never seen a child so young be so poised on the witness stand like I was.

Shortly after the trial, my family and I were at church. After the service had ended, we were preparing to leave... I looked up to see Donald looking in our direction with an odd grin on his face. I nearly lost my mind that day and my family had to calm me down. All I could think about was he got off and he is free as a bird after all he put me through and there he was grinning at me like nothing ever happened.

Some people were looking at me, probably wondering what was wrong with me... not knowing my story. In my mind, all I kept saying to myself was "How could this be?! That he is free to walk around and keep bringing back all these awful memories that would make me so nauseated to the point that I felt like throwing up?!" I should have received some type of counseling but all I ended up receiving was a heavy dose of low self-esteem and no one to talk to about what I was feeling. I was left to carry the burden of, "it's my dirty little secret"!

Even though years have passed, I have many gaps in my memories of what happened to me afterwards because I believe the only way I could deal with what happened to me was to try to forget it by suppressing those memories.

I only have vague memories of my father coming around on and off to visit us and did not really feel like he was there for me like a girl needs her dad to be for her. The experts say that the relationship between a father and daughter is crucial to how her image of what a healthy relationship should look like (the blueprint, basically).

A father should be there teaching how a woman should be treated and cherished but that was not what I saw as an example. I saw my mother struggling to provide for us while he was not there. I guess that is why I got so upset when my mother told me that she told my father about the man molesting me because I felt like he should have been there to protect me! My relationship with my aunt was destroyed and I truly resented her because I kept thinking she could have saved me from that monster. How could she have been so irresponsible as to turn over the care of her nieces to a stranger? She never showed any remorse towards me for her part in this whole mess. The thing that used to keep eating at me from the inside was after the trial, everyone acted like it was just a nightmare and it never actually happened, and that I was also supposed to pretend for the rest of my life! I just needed to talk about it to someone—anyone—but everyone was silent, so I kept silent.

Some years later, my dad would come back into our lives and my parents would tell me that we were moving to Maryland which was a big deal. Then, my parents told me, "You're about to have a new brother or sister on the way." The move turned out to be a big adjustment for me for many reasons but I started to feel better about it when my parents told me that they were going to put the baby's nursery in my room. As the months went on, they would purchase items for the baby and it was being stored in my room. I was terribly excited about the arrival of my new brother or sister and I could not wait.

I was so caught up with excitement of the upcoming event that I did not notice that my mom was going to the doctors quite frequently due to her diabetes. My mom's friends and members of the church threw her a baby shower, and all the items for the baby were set up in my room.

The special day came and my parents left for the hospital one evening. All day the next day, we were excited and waiting on the news from the hospital. Finally my dad called and I ran to the phone and I asked, "Well, what do I have... a brother or sister?" and he says the baby was stillborn. Then, confused, I asked: "It's still not here yet?" Then my father said she was born dead.

I felt devastated every time I would sit in my room and cry looking at all the baby stuff we had waiting for the baby and we never got to meet her. It was the first time I dealt with grief and I didn't know what to do with the pain so I did what I did as with everything else— buried the feelings inside and kept quiet about it.

Chapter 3

Identity Crisis

I truly struggled in school feeling like I was just going through the motions because I was doing what was expected of me and trying to live up to my mother's expectations. I found it hard to fit in, so I mostly kept to myself because the other children would find anything to make fun of me. They made fun of my unusual name many times, they also teased me about being heavy but the thing that really made me feel isolated was the color of my skin.

When I tried to gravitate to the groups of White children, they would say, "Don't come over here because you're Black." Then I tried to be included in the group of Black children. They said, "You don't belong over here because you're White," so I was shunned by both groups. One of the most hurtful experiences was when I had a puppy love friendship with this boy and we used to play on the playground together. I felt like I finally fit in somewhere and one day this little White boy ran up to the boy I was playing with and said, "Why are you playing with that Black girl?" The boy I was playing with said to the little White boy, "What are you talking about, she isn't Black." Then he turned to me and said, "Tell him…" I hung my head down and replied, "I am Black" in a low shameful tone and stood there while he walked away.

There I stood by myself feeling all alone again. At that moment, I had a flashback of the time my family traveled by car to visit my father's hometown Birmingham, Alabama. As we drove, we had to pass through Georgia and when we were entering the state, there was a huge billboard with the face of the then Governor George Wallace with words that said, "Go Home Niggers You Are Not Welcome Here". It was the first time I had ever heard the word so I had to ask my parents what it meant.

I was singled out as a constant target probably because I was a loner without a crew behind me. There were many times while riding the school bus, I would be attacked with crumpled up paper balls or spitballs being tossed at me, people hitting me, or saying mean jokes about my weight... it was so many demeaning things that I lost count.

There was one incident that made me make a stand for myself and declare I had had enough though. A classmate with a group following her came up to me and told me that after school that day, after getting off the bus, they were going to jump me. I tell you, when you hear people talking about beating you up, it paralyzes you with fear. That was what I went through. Just knowing that I had no clue how I would fight someone because I never been in an environment where I felt like needed to learn this skill. Even when I started to have problems in school, my mother attempted to try to teach me how to fight by having me to throw punches at a pillow. But I was smart enough to know what she tried to teach me wasn't going to work for this battle.

So all day I was praying in my head for an answer on how to get out of that fight but it didn't help that the word had spread and I could hear the other students saying, "Yeah, fight today after school" as soon as we get off the school bus. I was truly wishing the time would slow down but the next thing I knew, it was the end of the school day and we were headed toward the buses to load up for the different routes. I still hadn't figured out what I was going to do.

Everybody on the bus was whispering and laughing and kept looking towards my direction. Then the bus stopped to let us off at our stop. I grabbed my bookbag and started walking to the front of the bus and walked down the steps. Once everyone had gotten off the bus, they formed a circle and the next thing I knew I threw my bookbag down and I started screaming loudly while spinning around like the Taz the Tasmanian devil then I got in a crouching position then I saw people looking around at each other and they started backing up saying, "Hey everybody, she is crazy! Let's leave her alone," and everyone headed home. I looked up at the sky as I walked home, and I said, "God, thank You for what You just did for me!"

As the years passed, I could name on one hand the people I considered as my friends and I really did not look forward to high school either. While I was in high school, I was constantly bullied which really did not help my self-esteem. Most of the boys finally grew up by my senior year and that was when things started to feel better for me. I was accepted into the Work-Study program and I only had to attend 2-3 classes per day, and I started making my own money.

While working my Work-Study job, I met a guy who worked in the same area as my job and we became involved in a relationship that would lead to my first sexual experience. I can truly say nothing was good about it and I truly regretted it. I learned later on about his true character when I received a call from a woman claiming to be his wife. She went on to tell me that they had children together. The next day that I saw Victor, I told him, "Don't even speak to me anymore," and when he asked me why I told him that I received a phone call from his wife and she told me about their kids too. He tried to explain, and I just walked away. Whenever I would see him after that, I walked in the opposite direction.

Unfortunately, my mother's health got to the point where she couldn't work anymore so she applied to get Social Security. However, they kept denying her approval so she expressed her difficulties to her doctors who knew that she was medically unable to work anymore. All of my mother's doctors wrote letters to explain the extent of her medical issues and once she forwarded all the letters from all of her doctors to the Social Security Administration, they finally approved her Social Security benefits. Because it took them so long to approve, they ended up owing her lots of retroactive benefits as well as monthly benefits.

During my school years, I missed many days due to my mother's health issues and sometimes, she needed my help because the diabetes was wreaking havoc on her body. It was causing her to be so weak some days. My mother began teaching me how to pay the household bills. She would drill me many times on what to do when the money comes in for the month. Every time she would purchase money orders for the bills, she would have me fill them out so that I knew exactly how to do it. After my mom was confident that I had learned how to take care of the bills, she took the extra step and eventually made arrangements for me to have power of attorney so that should something medically happen, and she was unable to take care of things, I would have the legal ability to pay all the bills.

———— ꙮꙮꙮ ————

When I used to visit my godparents, there was a family that used to live next door. There was a guy that lived next door and we started hanging out together with some other friends. After some time, we ended up dating each other. I finally met someone who appeared to care for me, and he made me feel loved once we became intimate. As time went on, I started to talk to him about where he wanted to go with his future career. He said he was comfortable where he was and happy with his current position. I asked him if the company had offered him a management position and he said yes, they did, but he didn't want that position and that he would have to go to school. I didn't feel comfortable with that because I couldn't understand his fear of success so I left it alone.

I started to notice something was wrong with my boyfriend, and it began to get worse as time went on. We would make plans and I would wait hours for him and he wouldn't show up The next day I would be upset and ask him what happened to him and he would say he was hanging out with his boys and lost track of time but it kept happening more frequently. I thought that was the only problem I was dealing with until one day I was in the house watching out the window and I watched my man drink one beer after another until he eventually stumbled his way into his house.

Then, I found out he would go to the liquor store quite frequently and treat all his friends that didn't have money to buy drinks too. They would go to their hangout spot and drink all night. I used to think the only problem I would have to deal with was another woman—not his buddies. When I finally got to the point where I could not deal with the drinking anymore, I went to him and told him I was giving him an ultimatum: either he stopped drinking or I was going to break up with him. When I said it I really believed he loved me so much that he was willing to choose me over the drinking. However, I didn't understand that he was an alcoholic and could not stop without help... but I could no longer hang around to see him ruin his life, so I broke up with him!

After all my struggles and obstacles, I managed to graduate high school and only the good Lord knew how hard it was to get to the end. I decided to attend my local community college because the thought of taking the SAT was not a battle I wanted to tackle, and I knew it was not required to enter Prince George's Community College. Unfortunately, I got a low score in Algebra which was ironic since I knew it pretty well. I had to enroll in pre-Algebra class which I aced, and I even would come to the board to elaborate on things to the other students.

My major was Computer Science, and I was foolish enough to register for a 7 a.m. class knowing that I did not drive so I had to get up at 5 a.m. and take several buses. Introduction to Computers was my first class and I felt completely lost in the class. Each time the teacher spoke, I felt like he was speaking a foreign language. I finally went to the instructor after I failed the first test and explained to him that I needed help because I was not grasping the concepts that he was teaching us. He then told me he cannot really assist me because he never learned BASIC (the computer language) and I was floored so my next thought was "I am in trouble."

Then the instructor suggested that I see if some of the other students can assist me or maybe get a tutor. The thought of trying to befriend these computer nerds was overwhelming but still I tried and it was like being in school again trying to find a fit where nobody wanted to include you so it was an epic fail. I was confused at how the man who is the instructor of a basic computer is teaching a class he knows nothing about but brags about the computer company he owns. In my head, I was like, "He is a fraud!"

Since this was my major, I stayed in the class. He assigned us our first project and I was about to pull my hair out. I decided to go to the instructor again trying to get some assistance and what I got was him writing it out without telling me how he arrived at the answers which literally was of no help at all. For the rest of the class, I barely managed to get my head above sea level and then came the final and it bombed. My final grade was an F! I felt like a total failure and one of the worst things about it was that I sacrificed getting up at 5 a.m. taking those buses—just to fail and it was my major.

I did not need to know rocket science to figure out it was time to change my major and so before I signed up for my classes for the next semester, I changed my major to Business Management. While I was signing paperwork for my grant money during the start of the next semester, I noticed that I was eligible to apply for the Work-Study program so I applied. I was approved and I started working on campus. Once I started to feel comfortable during my second semester, I ventured around campus and I ended up signing up to be in the community college's gospel choir. It turned out to be a great fit for me. I finally found a group of people I could fit in with and it was fun.

The choir members hung out on campus but we also spent time together at outside events. I must add—we were really good and once, we were even invited to sing with a major gospel artist at one of his performances. Unfortunately, we would have too much fun sometimes and ended up missing some classes, but I very much enjoyed the experiences and the friendships I developed from it. We had some great concerts that would pack the auditorium and being a member of the choir led to many great memories.

I eventually realized that I needed to get focused on my classes again, so the next semester started with me getting a Work-Study job in the Business Department (which was my new major) and it ended up working to my advantage. Most of my instructors knew me so the downside of that was they would make it a point to call on me to answer questions about the assigned work quite frequently. Luckily, those classes were my strength.

As I went into my last year, I was taking the buses frequently back and forth to my classes so I started having conversations with this older gentleman—Luis—who drove the bus on the route I took. Because I used to sit in the front most of the time, we would have quite a few comments on some of the people and events that would happen on the bus. Eventually, we talked about other topics and what made the talks great was the fact he also had a great sense of humor. The most hilarious thing was watching people's reaction when they found out he was Hispanic because when you looked at him, you would have thought he was White especially since he also had steel blue eyes.

I started to stay on the bus beyond my stop to spend time with him and we would occasionally embrace one another from time to time. Eventually, Luis worked up the nerve to ask me out and since I didn't see any harm, I agreed to go out with him. When Luis took me out, I can truly say I was impressed because I had never been treated out like that by a man. I felt like a grown woman being treated like a queen down to the food and champagne that he ordered for us.

I was truly caught up in him and the fact that he was a complete gentleman was sealing the deal for me. We started to go out on a more frequent basis. This led me to deal with a tricky situation at home because my mother caught on that I was seeing someone. She wanted to meet him but how could I explain to her that he is the same age as her without WWI breaking out?! When I told Luis he was going to have to meet my mother, he was not excited about it of course, but I kept saying, "Just don't reveal your true age to her," and the whole time I'm thinking it was going to be pretty hard to conceal the fact that he is young with him being partially bald.

The meeting was not as bad as I thought it would be even though I was reading some of the looks she was giving him. There were no fireworks. Luis and I continued to date and he even let me talk to his daughter who was the same age as me which was kind of weird for me… then I started to notice something out of the ordinary when we would go out. When we went out, he would wait for his best friend or he would go to his best friend's house to pick him up and he would drive us to where we were going so my curiosity got the best of me and I asked him about it. He explained to me that he got a DUI and he was only supposed to drive to and from work. This revelation kind of shook me and the fact that he didn't tell me this left a little question mark in the back of my mind. When I thought back on it, it explained a lot though because his best friend had a family himself so many times we ended up over their house eating dinner. His wife was probably like *just invite them over so you wouldn't go out with them so much.*

I will never forget how he invited me over once to a big family gathering which was a bit of a disaster for me because I wasn't familiar with the food. I didn't want to eat it and they kept staring at me while speaking Spanish. One night, he took me to an apartment and we stayed there a while, talking and laughing. Just when it seemed that we were going to get intimate, he stopped and said not yet and I was like *what a gentleman.*

Later down the road we did become intimate and we tried some crazy things in some crazy places, but it did not matter because I was all caught up. One evening we were out and I was sitting in his car while he went into a store when I had this overwhelming intuition to open up his glove box and when I looked through it I started pulling out some mail that was addressed to him. However, it wasn't the same address as where he took me to so I quickly put it back without saying anything. For the rest of the night I thought to myself *should I or should I not say anything about what I saw*? After thinking about it overnight, I decided to ask him about it in a letter because I tend to express myself better in writing as opposed to talking in person or over the phone. People always say, "If you really don't want to know the truth then don't ask." Well I got on his bus route and handed him the letter but before I got off, I told him to read it and we can talk about when he picks me up the next day.

I never would have thought that I would get the answers he gave me. He started off by telling me that the apartment he took me to wasn't his—it was a friend's that let him use it. And then he said, "I have a house but the reason why I didn't take you there is because my daughter and her mother live with me." I felt like somebody had punched me in my chest and knocked all my breath out of my body. After he told me all of that, I told him to take me home because I needed to reevaluate if I was willing to stay in this relationship. I took a couple of days to myself but the bottom line, what I thought was *he is not married to her and he is good to me so I told myself that I could overlook this situation.*

In hindsight, I'm pretty sure he knew what I would end up doing and that's why he told me the truth. The young and dumb me who had never had a man treat her like he did was willing to put up with anything. The first time we were intimate again after finding out about the secret he kept from me, he told me that he loved me and wanted me to have his baby and it made me feel special. We were out riding to his best friend's house one day and we got into a big argument which got so heated that we ended up yelling at each other. He told me to shut up at one point and I told him, "Don't tell me to shut up," but I did eventually quieted down because I started to get nervous that we might have an accident while he was driving. It wasn't worth the risk.

I noticed that we were spending less time together but it turned out to be a blessing and it allowed me to reevaluate our relationship. I made a decision to end it so I called and told him. Several weeks later,

I noticed my period was late and I kept feeling fatigued so I followed my instincts to find the nurses' station on campus to request them to give me a pregnancy test. While the nurse was preparing the test, she started asking me some questions like: Have you been having unprotected sex? I said yes. She said, "So you were planning to get pregnant?" then I replied no. Then she said, "So you were setting a plan to self-sabotage yourself?" Then and I got quiet for a moment to think about what she said then I said, "I guess you are right." She gave me the test and then she looked at me and said, "Young lady, you are pregnant. You should follow up with your doctor to confirm."

When she said the last part, I barely heard her because I felt like I went numb and I walked around campus like a zombie—being physically there but mentally in another galaxy. I really had a hard time deciding what to do next because all I could think about was how Luis was going to take this news since I had clearly broken it off with him weeks ago. There I was, calling him out the blue to tell him he's going to be a father again. So after walking around in circles trying to get my nerves I finally searched for a payphone to call him with the news. In a way, I was glad when I got his answering service. I left a message hoping it would at least soften the blow as far as I was concerned because my heart was nearly beating out of my chest as I said the words "I am pregnant!"

Chapter 4

New Mother Decisions

I had so many decisions to make about my life and my baby's life but at that point, I didn't even know if Luis wanted to be in his child's life. I needed to talk to him first to see if he wanted to be in the picture. Luis finally called me, and we needed to have a discussion on what our next steps should be, so I brought up needing to make an appointment to go to the doctor. I made the appointment and let him know when it was and he picked me up for it. While we were on our way back to my house, I started discussing the fact that as time went on, I would be needing maternity clothes and since I was still in school and only had a part-time job, I would need him to help out financially.

That low-life creep told me, "You should apply to the Department of Social Services. All you have to do is tell them you don't know where I'm at and I will give you some money every now and then on the side." It took everything in me to keep from losing my cool with him, but I told myself to just keep quiet until I got home and come up with another plan. As soon as I got in the house, I called the Department of Social Services and requested paperwork so that I can report all his information. When I received the papers, I gave them all the information. It was humiliating enough to have to have to go and apply for assistance when he made good money to help take care of his child but instead, he would rather let me be on the State's dime.

Once I submitted the paperwork back, they in turn submitted his information to Child Support. When they sent me paperwork, I again gave all his information down to the color of his car. Our child deserved to have the best, not scraps, and if he thought I was going to settle for less than what we deserved, then he really underestimated me.

When I went to the doctors, they ran a battery of tests and I was at my Work-Study job when they called me with the results. First, they told me urine and blood showed high levels of sugar so they were recommending that I go get a glucose test at the high-risk clinic since I may have diabetes. Then they floored me when they told me I also tested positive for gonorrhea and I swear I saw red! The next thing I heard the doctor say was "You need to come in right away to take some medication." I was so angry that I wanted to find Luis and kill him so I had to talk to one of my co-workers to calm myself down. I couldn't figure out his schedule so I told myself *I know where he parks his car so I should go bust his windows out.*

I got to the clinic to take my medication and they said I needed to notify everybody that I have been with that I had gonorrhea. I said I was only with one person so I know he gave it to me so why should I tell him, and they were like, "You have to tell him." So I finally got in touch with him to tell him what the nurse said and he tried to act like he didn't know what I was talking about. Then he tried to make it like it was a joke, so I hung up on him.

The whole pregnancy was rough for me due to the diabetes and I ended up being hospitalized three times mainly because the stress of the pregnancy kept sending my blood sugar up. The doctors decided to bring me into the hospital so that they could get my blood sugar in control. The doctors were getting worried about the baby's health and his size because they told me diabetic mothers tend to have bigger babies. They decided that they wanted to deliver the baby early by C-section, but before determining when to set a date, they ordered an amniocentesis test to be done to check on the baby's lungs before they delivered him early. When the test results came back, it showed that my baby's lungs were good.

They set the day to deliver my baby and it ended up being the same day of my baby shower was scheduled for, so while they were having the shower for us, I was in the delivery room with my godsister by my side. The doctors were betting on how big he was going to be. My son Emmanuel (which means "God is with us"), was born on September 1st at 8 pounds and 15 1/2 ounces. It was really rough in the hospital after the C-section trying to recuperate because of the extreme pain, so the doctor ordered Demerol. Those shots hurt in the beginning before numbing the pain but the drawback was I hated the feeling that it gave. People were visiting me but later I would question myself... *was I dreaming or did I really see someone?* Because of the Demerol I was taking, they stopped letting me bring my son to my room because I would fall asleep with my baby in my bed, and they felt like it may lead to my baby getting hurt. After they did that, I decided to stop taking the Demerol and brace the pain with Tylenol. The next thing I knew was the hospital notifying me that they were going to release me to go home. Before I was sent back home, I had a minor breakdown and asked for someone to talk to me because I broke down in tears and was pacing the hospital room floor. The nurse began talking to me and asked me how was I feeling. When I was finally able to get out what I was feeling, she explained to me that I was experiencing what is called, "post-partum blues". My only comfort during that time was that my mother was there to help me understand some things about motherhood that I was not prepared for.

———————

I got home with the baby and made myself comfortable. Then I unpacked stuff from the hospital and decided to take a nap while my son was asleep. While I was resting, the phone rang and the person on the other end of the phone said they were calling from the dialysis center where mom was. She told me that my mom took ill and they had to rush her to the emergency room. I immediately jumped up to clear my head from my slumber and she told me that the hospital would be calling me shortly. I was sitting there looking at my baby like *what am I going to do with my baby on my own?!*

My mother's doctor called me some time later and told me that they would be keeping my mother for a couple of days to run some tests to find out what was causing her problems. The next days were rough because my son just kept crying and everybody was giving me suggestions on what to try and nothing was working. I was so tired because I wasn't getting any sleep since I was usually up all night walking around the house, rocking him—hoping and praying that he would stop crying so we could both get some sleep. Finally, after several nights of no sleep, I was complaining to my godmother about how exhausted I was. She suggested that the baby and I should come over to her house so she sent my godfather to pick us up.

It was a good thing my godmother had suggested we come over so she could help me out because I was truly at my wit's end. It was so bad that one night, because I was so exhausted from not being able to sleep because he was crying all night, I put him on the bed and just walked away. I paced around talking to God saying I couldn't take it anymore, and it was at that second I realized how much of a thin line it was between losing control and walking away until I gathered my thoughts and realized my baby had no clue as to what was going on.

My godmother was sent from heaven because when we unpacked, she said, "So this is what we are going to do... we are going to take care of him in shifts so you can go get some sleep. I will stay up and take care of him." So after days of no sleep, I was finally able to get some. Thanks to my godmother, I no longer felt overwhelmed. But the funniest thing was that the next day, my godsister said, "Lord after that baby cried all night, it makes me want to never have kids of my own," and we all had a good laugh about it.

Once the weekend was over, my godfather drove Emmanuel and me back home. Several days later, my mother was released from the hospital and this was where I found myself saying to myself, "Be careful what you ask for you might just get it." I was looking forward to my mom coming home thinking that she would be such a great help to me, but it turned out to be quite the opposite. I ended up feeling like I was taking care of two babies because even though she was home, she wasn't strong enough to help me out and she was dependent on me as well.

Several months later, paperwork from Child Support Enforcement came in the mail saying that I must show up for court to determine the paternity of Emmanuel. I took Emmanuel and my father drove us to court on the scheduled court date. After everyone checked in and sat down, the judge explained what the process was going to be. For instance, when your name was called and you were denying paternity, then you would make arrangements to pay for the DNA test that was over $100 at the time. If you were admitting paternity, then would step outside and make arrangements for setting up a payment amount. So I looked around and saw Luis sitting in the courtroom and after several names were called, they then called our names. I noticed that when he stood up, another man stood up too. That man spoke up on his behalf so the judge replied, "Shall I assume since you are representing Mr. Rodriguez that he will be denying paternity?" He replied, "Against my advice, he will be admitting to paternity today."

It took everything inside me to contain my anger. Just the sheer fact that he brought an attorney with him to try to deny our child angered me so much. The next step was for us to exit the courtroom to meet with a court-appointed mediator. We all sat down in a small cubicle with Luis, his attorney, myself, and Emmanuel. The woman looked at my son and then looked at Luis and said, "Your son looks just like you and there's no way you can deny him." She then began by putting in all of Luis's information and she asked where he worked. He said Metro and she was about to ask for the address but stopped herself and said, "Oh we already have the address (implying that they had many child support cases with METRO/WMATA)." The mediator then started to inquire about his salary. His attorney jumped in the conversation to interject that he is already paying child support for another child. My head almost snapped off my shoulder when I turned around to look at him to say, "How many kids do you have?!" and this fool started laughing and shrugging his shoulders like it was all a big joke.

My son was deprived of what he deserves because this man has spread his seed in many states. We started to discuss visitation rights and my anger started coming out when she told me I have to allow him to see his child. I quickly caught myself and said, "Sure, no problem. I know he will not visit him anyway." Years later, Luis and I had a conversation about him helping out more financially because I was struggling. His comment basically was "You are lucky you get what you're getting every month. You better not attempt to go to Child Support to get more because if you do, I will make sure what you are getting now will be reduced." Those words made me back down because the last thing I needed was to receive less.

One lesson I learned throughout this situation was no matter how negative it was between my son's father and me, my son didn't deserve to hear about how I felt his father was a deadbeat who had to be forced by the courts to support him. I never talked bad about his father to him or around him because I didn't want him to grow up to resent me for it. He was too young to know and understand our story.

Several years later, my son started acting out in school and I was called into a conference to discuss the issues they were having with him. I was referred to a guidance counselor who recommended I take him to see a therapist to talk to him about what was going on with him since he was not talking to me. I found a counselor and made an appointment for my son. Afterwards, the therapist and I had a conversation where she discussed with me that he was acting out because he doesn't have a relationship with his father.

This is for all the women who say I can raise my son all by myself and I don't need no man to help me... please stop telling yourself that lie because you will do a disservice to your sons. Please don't get me wrong—if your child's father is abusive or a negative influence, by all means separate yourself from them. But there are alternatives, because no matter how much we do as mothers, some things we can't teach a boy about being a man.

I was faced with a tough decision to put aside how I felt about Luis and how our relationship turned ugly over the fact that my son needed to connect with his father since they never developed a relationship. Even though some people advised me not to do it, I decided it was worth it to help my son. So, I contacted his father and told him his son needed him to come around and spend some time with him. His father started coming around and spending time with him and it seemed like things were going well until I started to notice his father was acting like he wanted to rekindle something between us. I told him that this was about our son, not us being together.

Now ladies, take note of what happened next… one day, Luis came by and he had been drinking—I didn't catch on until my son came to me and he was really upset. It was at that time that I explained some of the reasons why his father and I weren't together. He then understood why his father hadn't been around in the past. On one of Luis's visits, he saw a male friend of mine come by my house. He questioned who my friend was as though he had a right to inquire about anyone in my life. He got upset and said if I had my friend coming around, why did he have to be there. I told him he was there to spend time with his son.

After that, he stopped coming around. I then had to deal with my son who had just started having a relationship with his father, and then he dropped out of the picture. I felt so much guilt because I started questioning myself. I was asking myself, "Should I have ever brought him into the picture at all?" I observed that my son wasn't as upset as I thought he would be but I think if I never made the effort to let him meet him, it would have hurt him more in his future.

As a mother, I had to acknowledge the fact that he needed a positive male in his life. I decided to pull some men in my family who represented strong positive role models such as my Uncle Mike. He had been a man who my son looked up to. Then I pulled in the resources of my church family who started a male mentoring program. They formed a circle of support for me. Prayer was a major influence during those times, and it helped keep me going because as a single parent, it was tough. I lived in a rough part of town and it had lots of negative influence all around. My son could have easily got caught up in it, but God kept a fence around my son.

My son desired most of the same things other young men his age wanted—like expensive tennis shoes. I remember a conversation we had about some tennis shoes he had his eyes on and when he told me how much they cost I was like, "No way." I said, "If you want those, you better get a job and make that money for them." My son truly outsmarted me, and not only did he find a job that was close to home so he could ride his bike there, but he was able to get free food there as well. I was so grateful that my son had developed a desire to want to work and earn his own money to get what he wanted.

When my son got to high school, we discussed what he wanted to do beyond high school and he mentioned that he was thinking about going to the police academy. Since my son had kept a job while in high school, he was able to split the costs for his prom, senior fees, and his cap and gown for his graduation with me which was a blessing. Everything seemed like it was rolling along all smooth until one day, my son came home from school and I saw that he had this woman in uniform with him. I was puzzled as to who she was. Then, he introduced me to this lady and said she was from the United States Marine Corps. I still didn't understand why she was in our home until he said, "Mom, I have decided that I want to enlist in the Marines." I looked at this woman, then back at my son, then I said, "Excuse me ma'am, I need to have a conversation with my son."

I had to take a seat and get my thoughts together because I was so surprised. I didn't know how to act because he never discussed having a desire to enter the military. Finally I asked him, "Where is this coming from all of a sudden?" He began to tell me that the recruiters were at his school and they had a talk with them and he decided it sounded like something he wanted to do. I shook my head and said, "You talked to them, and after talking with her, you know this is something you want to do?" He said, "Yes, mom!"

I was furious! All I could think about was *this woman probably gets a commission on how many children she can sign up* and *I am sure she is pretty aggressive on how they persuade these students to join.* I told him I would have to think on it because the other thing that got me mad was, he is a minor. Before she had any discussion with him, I should have been present.

We had several discussions about his coerced decision to join the military after that day. I decided he should invite the recruiter to the house so we could address my questions and point out some things that my son probably didn't bring up when they initially had their conversation. I will admit, even before the woman arrived; I was very defensive in my thoughts because I did not appreciate how it was handled. The recruiter was also prepared and well trained as I detected, and at the end of the conversation, my son was still set on the idea of going into the military. I ended up inquiring as to what the next steps were and she mentioned him setting an appointment to take the ASVAB test.

Once my son went to his appointment to take the test, the ball started running pretty quick. Then, something interesting came up. They told my son that since he was a minor, he would have to have permission from both of his parents. My son and I started to laugh because we hadn't heard from his father in years. We let the recruiter know that we had no way of reaching him so we had to sign a waiver to get him in. The next thing I knew my son was being sworn in and had a date when he would be reporting for boot camp after his graduation.

Before graduation though, there was prom. It was exciting to see him get ready for it but it became immediately sour for me. After prom, my son decided that he wanted to stay out. Then he started staying at his friend's house, so he could, I guess, be independent of his mother before he left for the military. The most hurtful part was that Mother's Day came and went and he didn't call me. In desperation, I reached out to his recruiter to talk to him about the situation. This woman came through for me. She got in touch with my son and told him he better get in touch with me every day.

Then, one day I got a call from a hospital to tell me that my son had come to the emergency room for an injury and they needed permission to treat him. I gave my permission then headed up to the hospital. On my way there, I got lost so it took me a long time to get there. because I am known to easily get lost even when given directions.

When I finally arrived and as I was entering the hospital, my son was leaving with his best friend's dad. I looked at him and said, "This is my son, so this is between us, and he is coming home with me tonight." He backed down. I stopped at an all-night drugstore to get the medicine he needed for the pain and then I asked him what happened. He said they were in the park and he decided that he was going to swing on a vine like Tarzan and he swung right into the trunk of a tree. His crazy thought process landed him with broken ribs.

We headed home so I could get him comfortable. I had to get up early the next morning for work. I checked on him to make sure he was okay before leaving for work and after work, I headed home only to arrive to an empty house. He was gone again.

One of the consequences of my son's actions was he had to report the injury to his recruiter and he had to be examined by the military doctors before reporting in since he was due to report in a couple of weeks. The next week, I heard that my son was in a car accident and luckily, there were no major injuries. When I spoke to him hearing the news I said, "Boy, God is trying to tell you something!" After some time, he passed the medical exam that the military doctors gave him, and he was on his way.

Chapter 5

Mom's Last Goodbye

In the midst of my son being born, my mother's health was deteriorating and she was dealing with kidney failure. She needed to go on dialysis three times a week at a specialized facility. It was a scary time in the beginning because the doctors had to insert a device called a shunt and its purpose was to allow my mom to be hooked up to a dialysis machine. Because it is like having a foreign object in your body, it does not always have a smooth outcome. She suffered tremendous pain after it was inserted and she would moan and cry because of it. It was hard to see her going through such a hard time and not be able to help her out of the misery.

Later, one of her doctors suggested an alternative to the traditional treatments. She could do in-home dialysis which would require me to take a quick training course at the hospital to learn how to administer the treatments to my mom at home. That didn't work out too well for us because my mom kept getting infections even though we attempted to take every precaution that was taught to me. The doctors surmised that the house wasn't sterile enough for her treatments. They told us she had to get her treatment from a dialysis facility as soon as possible.

I had to split my time between my son and my mom. I went back and forth trying to take care of both of them (mom in the hospital and my son in the house) and sometimes, I got so tired because it was overwhelming carrying the load of responsibilities that was on my shoulders. There were many nights I found myself crying to God to give me strength to carry on from day to day. To top it off, I was also dealing with another sickness in the household. My sister kept disappearing from home due to her drug addiction. I really needed my sister's help financially since I wasn't working and I used to wait for her part of the money towards the bills on her payday. She would either show up empty-handed that evening or days later with no explanation.

It was becoming more difficult at home. My mom had a bad fall trying to go to the bathroom without calling my sister or myself to help her. Things became even harder when the doctors set my mom's ankle it wasn't done correctly. This resulted in an infection setting in and it had started moving up her leg. The doctors decided that the best course of action was to stop the infection by amputating part of her leg under her knee. They came to me with what they wanted to do because they needed me to sign the paperwork to do the procedure.

It was one of the hardest things I had to do but it had to be done to save her life. After the surgery, I got really messed up because my mother told me she could hear them sawing part of her leg off even though she was supposed to be under sedation. At one point, all the suppressed anger I had towards my aunt resurfaced because my aunt was a nurse and when my mom lost part of her leg, I needed help to lift her in and out of bed. My aunt wouldn't even come over to help me! She just called on the phone to tell me what to do. Eventually, my mother got fitted for a prosthetic leg. It initially caused her much pain at first until she got used to it.

My mom was used to being a very independent person who always did things for herself. She had a hard time adjusting to having to depend on her daughters to do everything for her because she had become weak and ill. My godmother was a lifeline because she came over from time to time to sit with my mom to give me a much-needed break. During those times, I thought to myself how shameful it was that my mom's siblings wouldn't come over to see her or just come sit with her to help me out. It seemed like I was never able to rest because as soon as one situation would ease up, there would be something else to deal with.

—⁓∽◦◦◦◦◦◦∽⁓—

I found out that during some of those times that my sister would go missing, she was at the house of her boyfriend's parents sleeping off her high. She was so caught up in her addiction that she didn't even care that she was causing more stress to me. I was so tired of all the times that my sister would go missing. Once, she was gone for several days. When my father and I drove around the neighborhood looking for her, we spotted her walking up the street towards our house with no shoes on. We coaxed her into the car and I remembered asking her where her shoes were. She finally told me she ran out of money for more drugs so she sold her shoes to get more.

After that incident, I decided to practice some tough love by taking her house key. I told her if she came back late, she wasn't getting in until the next day. The next time she went out and came back, I didn't open the door to her because I felt like it was becoming a safety issue. I had no idea who she was hanging around with or what she would do around my son while she was high. It was a tough controversial decision that I was forced to make because I had to make my son and my mom's safety a priority.

The other serious thing about my sister's situation was that her diabetes was uncontrolled. She didn't take the necessary medications which put her health at an extremely dangerous level. When my sister called me to ask if she can come home, I told her, "Since you keep running to the streets, you need to stay out there and you can come by to pick up your personal belongings during the day." My hurt over my sister's plight turned to anger when my godmother called me to tell me to please let my sister come back home, "for my mother's sake." At first, I truly didn't understand the whole meaning of what she was saying until she went on to tell me that my mother called her from the hospital. She said my mother told her that my sister came to the hospital to see my mother and told her about me kicking her out of the house. She started crying to my mother saying she didn't have anywhere to go.

I was furious because I felt like *why would you go up there and bother our mom about this situation?!* My mom didn't know about everything that had been going on with her because my mother needed to be stress free so she could heal quicker. Basically, my sister used my mother to get herself back in the house knowing that I would do anything to keep my mom happy.

The whole situation made me have flashbacks of when we were younger, and my sister would almost always find a way to get away with stuff just because she was the youngest. Our relationship was rocky after that and I told her she would have to go to some type of rehab to deal with her addiction problems. She did go to many programs and kept on relapsing. Some people who didn't know the whole story of what I had been dealing with or how it was to deal with a person who has an addiction thought I was the meanest person in the world, but I didn't care what people thought of me. They can walk a mile in my shoes *and then* let's see if they wouldn't feel the same way.

I remember my sister inviting me to an outpatient drug counseling session for my family and the counselor asked about how we felt about my sister. When they got to me, I said I don't trust her and others who were there mumbled disapprovingly under their breaths. The counselor replied, "You're absolutely right because addicts lie and cannot be trusted especially when under the influence." I looked around the circle of family and close friends as if to say thank you to the counselor because I was finally validated for feeling the way I felt.

My sister relapsed several times and usually, she ended up seeking out the same guy every time. She eventually became pregnant by this man, and then we got her back to an outpatient rehab center to start the process all over again.

When Emmanuel was about six months, I was introduced to a man named Thomas. He was the cousin of my godsister's boyfriend. We talked on the phone and eventually ended up going out a couple of times which was great to have an outlet from everything going on in my life at the time. However, I couldn't really devote time to a relationship with all the responsibilities I had on me at the time. We saw and spoke to each other occasionally, but nothing more developed.

Sometimes my mother would get close to death while hospitalized that her doctors would call me and tell me to gather the family and come quickly because she may not make it through the night. I would get my sister up and call my father to take us up to the hospital. My father used to get on my nerves because he would start crying so bad. I used to tell him to just stay in the waiting area while I go in because my mother didn't need all that crying when we came there to uplift her—not to depress her. He was such a weak man and no real support for me at all.

I had an idea to put my son's picture up on her IV pole so she would see it as soon as she opened her eyes, and she would get better. I really believed that my son being born kept my mother going longer because she loved him so much but sometimes, she would come home so weak that she couldn't hold him. I would just lay him on her chest she would talk to him, look at him and smile.

She developed a problem after being on dialysis, and for a while they were running out of places to put the shunt. They told her they needed to move it to her neck. She protested and said, "Absolutely not!" The doctors said if they did not make this move, she would not live long. My mom told the doctors and me that she was tired of being cut on and that she had enough.

My uncle—her youngest brother—had been helping me look for a nursing home that she would go to when she left the hospital. The doctors had explained to me that I would no longer be capable of administering the care she was going to need. The hardest part was when I told my mother that she was going to a nursing home, she got angry and she said, "If you do this to me, I will never forgive you!" The guilt was eating at me and it also was about to become a major financial burden for me because the nice place we found after a long search would require payment through her Social Security check. Unfortunately, that money was what paid the rent for our apartment. Arrangements were ready for my mom when she would get strong enough to leave the hospital.

———⁓⦵⦵⦵⦵⁓———

I remember the last day I saw her very clearly. My father had taken Emmanuel and me to church and we had made a plan to go up the hospital to see my mom. Afterwards, we were going out to eat. We followed our plan and we went to the hospital. When I got to my mom's room, it was really cold and quiet. I sat by her bed and talked to her but she never woke. I knew that they had been keeping her so heavily sedated since the doctors had performed the surgery against her wishes so I decided to let her rest. As I was leaving, I leaned down to give her a kiss on the forehead and I noticed she was cold so I pulled up the sheet to cover her up more and I told my mom goodbye. My father took us out to dinner at a restaurant and then he took us home. When I walked through the door, the phone was ringing off the hook. When I answered the phone I heard my godmother's voice on the other end and she sent my body numb when I heard her say those unforgettable words… "Your mother has died."

I was in complete denial I just kept saying it can't be true because I was just at the hospital to see her and she was asleep! The more we talked the initial shock started to wear off a little. I started to rethink my visit to the hospital and I started to believe that when I had last visited her, she was already gone. It would explain why she never woke and she was cold! It is because of this that I believe that the time of death listed on her death certificate is incorrect…

I thought back on the whole situation. I felt that God was merciful to us all. She was tired and ready to go to a place with no more pain and I wouldn't have to live with the guilt of putting Mom in the nursing home. I also reflected on a time where one of her doctors told me: "Because of all the times I had to call you and tell you to gather the family because I believed she wasn't going to make it through… your mother would make a liar out of me every time and because of that, she made me believe there is a God!" Even though some people had negative comments and thoughts about me because I had a child out of wedlock I know my son was a lifeline for my mother. I believe she hung in there through the pain because she wanted so badly to enjoy time with her grandson. I thank God every day that I didn't abort him. I had to get past all of the shock, grief, and pain to take control of the situation because I couldn't count on my drug addicted sister or weak ass father!

My mother's youngest brother Michael stepped up once again and took over the funeral arrangements. I was crying so much during that time that one morning, I woke up with both of my eyes almost swollen shut! Michael and his wife Tootie took Emmanuel and kept him for me so I could get a break while taking care of any last-minute funeral arrangements. It was my responsibility to call all the family to make sure they knew the dates and times of the wake and funeral. It was tradition to have the wake at night and then the funeral which I dreaded having to get the strength to attend the wake that night and the funeral the following day. I had to ask my aunt (my mother's sister) if we could use one of her burial plots to bury my mother since money was really tight. She agreed, but she claimed it was a clause attached to the plot that my mother had to have a Catholic funeral. It was weird because my mother had left the Catholic church so many decades ago.

I found out after the funeral that she made up that condition and when my uncle went to the church to finalize the arrangements, he had requested the priest not spray the smoky ashes at the funeral. My aunt who was a nurse by profession never came around to help me with my mom the whole time she was sick, but now she wanted to start trying to run things. She wanted to dictate what clothes my mom should be buried in. I never forgot how she brought a set of clothes that she suggested my mom be buried in and handed to my uncle. As soon as she went away, my uncle dropped those ugly clothes on the ground and then he ran over them and I laughed so hard.

The rest of my mother's siblings were acting like they were all broke and could not afford to contribute any money toward the funeral. On the night of the wake, we all gathered to go to the church. I took a deep breath and I walked up to the casket and viewed my mother's body. I was not pleased at the job that the funeral home did on my mom's body. I stayed in the back of the church with my uncle Mike and he was a ball of nerves while the service was going on.

Family and friends came and went throughout the night, but it was basically all a blur to me. Somehow, I made it through this night and the worst part was yet to come. I just wanted to go to sleep and wake up to see that it was all a dream!

On the day of the funeral, I felt like a zombie just going through the motions. The family was supposed to meet at my uncle Mike's house and the limousine was picking everyone up from there to take us to church. It was a good feeling when I walked into my aunt and uncle's house. My aunt Tootie was a godsend to me and my son during that awfully sad and painful time. While we were waiting for the rest of the family to show up, my aunt shared with me an experience that happened earlier that morning with my son while they were getting him ready for the funeral.

She told me that they were in their bedroom changing my son's diaper when he looked up to the ceiling and said, "Hi grandma." Then he moved his head from one point to the other as though he was following her around the room and then when his eyes stopped at where the window was, they heard him say, "Bye grandma," as he waved in the same direction. She told me my uncle and she both looked at each other and they were really freaked out but what was really crazy was that he was so young and my mom was so sick most of the time since he was born and she really didn't have a chance to bond with him like she wanted to.

I had heard in the past that children are sensitive to spiritual beings so even though I was amazed when I heard what happened, I believed it. When all the greetings and hugs had been passed around to the family, we all loaded up in the limo. I was in a fog the whole ride there. I was a little disappointed that my godmother was not there for me to lean on for support. We got to the church and we were escorted to the front of the church. The service began and I was not prepared for all the rituals that the priest performed during the service—neither was my uncle Mike. When they started spraying those ashes we were choking and my aunt was sitting behind me and I heard my uncle say, "I told them I didn't want all this shit"! The next thing I heard was my aunt Tootie trying to calm him down. Then, I looked behind me to see him about to get up from his seat. I knew wasn't going to go well inside this church.

I thanked God for my friend and angel Precious Rich who I had asked to sing for my mom's funeral because as soon as she started to sing, "I'm Going Up to Yonder", it began to soothe the savage beast that was stirring inside my uncle. He began to calm down and I breathed a sigh of relief! I made it until the end of the service without breaking down but I didn't make it out the church because as soon as we were instructed to stand up to leave and we were following behind the casket that was when the waterworks started. As I turned to walk out the front of the church, I saw my godsister Wonnie crying too!

The ride to the cemetery was a blur and I was just doing what was expected of me. We headed to the house afterwards and I was so drained. All I wanted to do was fall into my bed and sleep. My uncle Daniel followed me home and he kept looking around the house for some food. I told him that nobody had bought any food to the house so he would go home. I was so glad that my aunt and uncle had offered to keep Emmanuel for me at their house for another night so that I could get some real sleep. In order to get my Uncle Michael to agree to help me with the funeral expenses I had to agree to pay him back. Everything that was given to me at the funeral monetarily, I handed to my uncle to reimburse him for what he put out in advance for my mom's funeral.

Truth be told, I really could have used some of that money to help me out until we came up with a solution to the dilemma of how we were going to pay the next months' rent…

Chapter 6

Vulnerable Life Lessons

W hen I woke up the next day and my mom was dead and buried, I had to figure out what I was going to do financially because I had stopped working to take care of my mom. Then she was gone. All those years that my mom had tried to teach me things about the bills and how to take care of a household was obviously because she knew she wouldn't be here long. And to think I was so resistant learning these things because all I could think of was how much I was missing out on the things that other teenagers my age were doing!

I found myself living in a new reality that hit me like a brick to the face. At 23, I was on my own and I had to grow up even quicker. I knew I needed to come up with a plan. Because I had stopped working to take care of my mother, and it was going to take time to transition back to work. I talked to my godmother and she suggested that I talk to my father and ask him if he could move in and help me with the rent and other household bills until I got back on my feet. It was not an easy decision for me to let my dad move in because I have a lot of bad memories of how my dad treated my mom before she divorced him.

I was old enough to remember how I felt so angry at my father because I viewed him as a very weak man who could not handle my mom's illness. He would run over to his aunt's house many times instead of coming home while we would be waiting for him to come home with groceries. He didn't come home until the next evening, and when he did, he was empty-handed with no explanation. My father had no idea how much I knew about his past. Some of it was told to my mom by his family when we visited them in Birmingham, his hometown.

He was in the military before he met my mom and was supposedly dishonorably discharged when he served during the Korean War, because he impregnated a native woman. His family handed my mother pictures of my dad holding the son he had with the woman. That was when I found out I had a brother out there somewhere. After some years, he and my mom were married. A friend of the family got him a job with a very stable company named WSSC (Washington Suburban Sanitation Commission) and the job came with full benefits. However, he did not stay long because my father didn't like going to a nine-to-five job and he quit. The worst part of him quitting the job was that the health insurance was dropped and he didn't even have the decency to inform my mom. She found out when she went to a scheduled doctor's appointment only to be told they couldn't see her because she no longer had insurance coverage.

My father was more comfortable with a flexible schedule and so he ended up taking a job as a calendar salesman. He could start as late as he wanted and stay out late too. The thing that made my mom say, "this is enough" came many years later when this woman kept calling our house for my father but she never left a message. This continued for about a week. One day, the woman called again asking for my father but this time, she wanted to leave a message. She said, "Please tell Mr. Cox to get in touch with me at the police department." She left her name along with her phone number. I practically ran to relay the message to my mom and all I could think about was looking forward to eavesdropping on that conversation when my father got home.

Unfortunately, that got delayed because my father decided to pull one of his disappearing acts over his aunt's house again—or so I thought. Several days later, the phone rang one night and when I answered, I recognized my father's voice. I called my mom to answer the phone while I strained my ear to try to overhear the conversation to no avail. Then, I heard the receiver hang up. I waited a few minutes before asking who was on the phone. My mother replied, "You already know it was your father." I asked, "Where is daddy?" and she floored me with "Your father is in jail!"

I was so surprised that I didn't dare ask any more questions. I found out several days later that the phone calls from the policewoman were for my father to turn himself in because he had been caught shoplifting on tape several times. My mom might have forgiven him but she found out he got a light sentence because he told the police that he was selling the items he was stealing so that he could purchase food for his family. Basically, he lied.

The following week, my father called from jail. This time, I overheard the conversation and he said he was being released the next day. My mom's response was "Okay, when you get here your belongings will be outside in a box in front of the door. Also, the locks will be changed." I don't even know when my mom got the divorce but she had made up her mind that she was done and even though the ministers and church members advised her not to go through with it, many people didn't know all that she had endured. At the end of the day, she made a decision to do what was best for our family.

It was close to the time that my father was supposed to move in that I found out that he was seeing this woman. I started thinking to myself *what is he going to do about her* and then I find out through my godmother that he was planning to move her into our apartment too. The whole time my sister and I were preparing for him to move in, not once did he call me to discuss the fact that he planned on bringing this woman along. All the information I got about this woman was coming from my godmother—not my father—and I shouldn't be surprised because I can't remember the last time my father showed any resemblance of a backbone when it came to dealing with anything involving me and/or my sister.

I was dealing with the loss of my mother while trying to make adjustments mentally and physically. With my dad moving in soon, I had to deal with my father bringing another woman into the apartment that my mom had furnished. It was a really hard pill to swallow for my sister and me especially since my father never took the time to sit down with us and discuss the arrangement. The fact that he never considered our feelings was hurtful.

This woman came into our apartment with her nose up in the air as if she was bringing in some great possessions of her own and she had the nerve to come with an attitude that she was better than us and she wasn't even working. My father brought with him a very messy situation that just built up lots of resentment in the house. The good thing that happened is that my sister finally cleaned up her act by getting off the drugs. It was so many wars going on between my sister and me and my father's girlfriend Martha because she kept walking around like she was some kind of queen even though she was the only one in the house not working to contribute to the household bills. She constantly agitated arguments and one time, my son called me at work to tell me something was going on at home but could not talk because they were around. When I got home, I started fussing at him for calling me at work. He told me that my sister and Martha got into a big argument. I asked my father what happened and he told me my sister called Martha a bitch because she did not want my father to give my sister a ride somewhere. My sister and Martha got to swinging at each other inside the car!

My sister ended up moving out into a shelter because the atmosphere in the house had become so toxic. One night before my sister moved out, I was laying on my bed in my room when I heard loud voices coming from the kitchen. I quickly went down the hallway to the kitchen where I saw my sister holding an iron over Martha's head, threatening to bash her in the face. I started yelling, "What is going on" and my sister replied, "I'm sick of her calling me a drug addict." To make things worse, Martha said, "You are nothing but a drug addict." At that point I saw something change in my sister's eyes and she was aiming directly for Martha's head so I started yelling at her to stop. She was not hearing me anymore so I had to literally jump in between them and pull on my sister's hands to make her stop.

I later on found out that Martha used to practice witchcraft when my father met her but I only found this out after I came home one day to find little strips of colored material around and under my mattress. I could not figure out where it came from until I was having a conversation with my godmother. I mentioned what I discovered in my room. She then replied, "Oh no, I told her not to do that..." I asked her what she meant, and she told me that Martha told her she wanted to do something to make me like her. When Martha told my godmother what she wanted do, my godmother told her that that wasn't how she should go about it. Obviously she determined she was going to go back to her witchcraft days and tried to cast some kind of spell on me.

I got off that phone call with my godmother so fast and I stomped down the hall to their bedroom. I pounded on the door but lucky for her she wasn't there. I was pacing back and forth because I was furious. First, for invading my privacy by coming in my room and second, for trying to do some witchcraft on me. I started to calm down and I went to my room so I could pray to God to calm me down because I was about to hurt Martha real bad. The prayer worked and by the time she got home I told her, "Don't you ever come in my room again or it's going to be a major problem," and I walked back to my room.

In the middle of all the craziness in the house, I met Doug. We went out from time to time. He was this fake Muslim guy and the reason why I say that is because he really didn't practice any of their beliefs especially protecting their women. He was a straight out user and since I was in another valley mentally as far as my low self-esteem was concerned, I allowed him to mistreat me mentally and sexually. Then, I found out I was pregnant.

That was the first time I felt like my only option was to abort the baby, but this was a hard decision because I always felt like that that decision is considered to be murder in the eyes of God. I decided to confide in my pastors because they were also good friends of mine. My pastors advised me not to get an abortion. I remember the pastor's wife said to me, "If you get this abortion, you are going to get pregnant again." When I finally decided to tell Doug the news, he truly showed his cowardly behind by saying to me, "Well, you are on your own cause I'm leaving town." I just shook my head and then he said, "If you decide to get an abortion, I will help you out with the cost." Sad, but I wasn't surprised.

I went back and forth in my mind about what I was going to do about the baby. I just kept saying to myself that I hated living with my father and Martha so there was no way that I would bring my baby into this horrible atmosphere. After a month, I did my research to find an abortion clinic and made calls to find out what it was going to cost. When I had all the information, I tried to contact Doug, and of course he was nowhere to be found. Luckily, I had some money saved up. Because I knew my time was limited, I had to hurry up and schedule an appointment.

I told my father that I needed a ride to my appointment. It was really hard not to confide in anyone about where I was going but I was too ashamed to tell anybody. My father took me to the clinic and once inside, I picked up the necessary paperwork, filled it out, and returned it to the designated basket. I sat back down in the waiting area until they called my name. While I was seated, I looked around the room at the other women there and all of a sudden, what I was about to do started to sink in and all the emotions hit me at once. All the tears that I had been holding back began to flow. It felt like a dam had burst.

As I looked around, the women looked as if they were waiting to go to the movies or something and inside my head, I was screaming *we are about to kill our babies*. I felt like I was about to lose my mind because the very thing I had judged other women for, I was about to do with my body and it was tearing me up on the inside. Then, I heard the nurse call my name. I took a deep breath so I could get myself together to walk to the desk. I was motioned to take a seat. She then reminded me of the fee for the doctor's services and then I pulled out the cash. The nurse told me they didn't accept cash. I was like, "No one explained that over the phone when I made the appointment." She apologized, then mentioned getting a money order which was a problem for me, so I had to reschedule the appointment.

It was such an overwhelming process, and then I had to pick my emotionally damaged self up to do it again. By the time I was able to get another appointment, I had gone into another month of my pregnancy so the fee had gone up. At that point, mentally, I was a train wreck waiting to happen and waiting for the next appointment was not helping the situation. When the appointment finally came, I was barely keeping my emotions intact. This time around, the tears did not flow because I had already cried so many, but I just went through it mindlessly. When the nurse called my name, I gave her the money order. The next step was to go in the room, get undressed and wait for the doctor. As I laid on the table my nerves were bothering me so bad that I began to feel like I was going to throw up...

When it was finally over, and my father drove me home in complete silence. When I got home, I could not wait to get in my bed so I could ball up in the fetal position and cry myself to sleep. While I laid there, I asked God to forgive me for killing my unborn child. I pleaded with Him to help my mind. The next day when I woke up, I was still an emotional mess. I received a phone call from someone who was offering me a job.

It was like a wake-up call that I could move on with my life and that I should get this job so that I could have a new start and get back on my feet. The next day, I got dressed and went to the interview. They told me that they would be deciding later in the day. I received a call from the employer saying they wanted to offer me the position and I was grateful to God that in spite of my mess ups He still allowed a door to open for me. I truly believed if I hadn't got hired when I did, I would have slinked down in a deep depression.

The following week, I was chilling in my room when my father knocked on my door and told me that someone was at the door for me. On my way to the door, I was like *who it could be?* I was truly surprised to see Doug standing there. He said, "Hey" and I was like, "What do you want?" so he was like, "Can we talk?" I nodded and told him, "Let me get my shoes and I will be downstairs in a minute." I followed him to where he parked his car. When I and sat down in his car, he asked me how I was doing and started apologizing for not being around lately. The whole time I was just listening in silence. Then he started telling me that after I told him I was pregnant, he really wasn't ready to handle the announcement that he was going to be a father so that's why he didn't want to be around for me.

Doug continued talking about how he talked to several guys about the situation and how after talking to them, he realized he needed to be a man about the situation and be there to support me. It was at that moment that I truly believe I had a moment of insanity because all I remember is just swinging my fists at him uncontrollably. I didn't stop until he grabbed my hands and asked me, "What the hell is wrong with you?!" I turned to look him squarely in his face and replied, "Now you are ready to be a father?! Well it's too damn late because there is no more baby because I had an abortion!"

Then with all the strength left in my body, I exited his car to go back to my apartment. Several days later I would receive a call from Doug asking if we could still get together and my broken self said we could try. It didn't go well between us because every time I was with him, it was like a gigantic elephant in the room with a mental picture of me aborting our baby. I finally decided to end our so-called relationship because it was mentally toxic.

The new job became my focus to get over that whole mess. From time to time, I would stop by a little sandwich shop in the mall—mostly after work but sometimes for lunch too. I developed a friendship with a guy named Chris who worked there. He would always crack jokes and he kept me laughing all the time which I truly needed since I was still dealing with all the craziness at home. We eventually exchanged numbers and started going out. Looking back, I feel this was a rebound relationship that should have never happened. The self-defeating prophesy would come to pass just like my pastor's wife said. I got pregnant by Chris and he turned into an annoying monster. He was very controlling at times which drove me crazy on top of dealing with everything else.

Whatever happened in this crazy relationship, one thing for sure was that I was not having an abortion. He tried to talk me into having one but my mind was made up. He really started tripping because he would call me and say, "Where you been?" and would I would say, "I just got home from work." Then he would question me as to why it took me so long to get home since he had developed a timeline of how long it should take me to get off the bus and then walk into my house. It got so bad and I told him I needed a break from him but instead, he got worse. He would call me over and over again to the point that my sister would come over and try to talk to him over the phone and ask him to stop calling me for a while to give me a break.

One day I came home and discovered that the electricity was off and I couldn't figure out why so I waited up for my father to discuss it with him. He acted like he didn't have a clue so the next day, I took matters into my own hands by calling the electricity company myself which was easy to do since the bill was in my name. When I got through to the company, they told me they had issued a turn off notice due to non-payment. The worst part was that this went against my credit since the bill was still in my name. I talked to my father about the bill and he said he didn't have the money to pay for it but he mentioned that I could pay for it with my income tax money. I figured out that that's why he didn't pay it.

A decision needed to be made about the bill getting paid. My son and I were having to eat out every day, and it was the summertime... without air conditioning... while dealing with my pregnancy. While I thought about what I was going to do about the outstanding bill, I spoke to my pastors and they said, "Don't use your money for the bill especially since he agreed to pay the bill. You can come stay up here in the air conditioning as much as you want." I wrestled with the decision all day and that night, I had a seriously real dream. It shook me into action and help me make up my mind that I was not going to pay that bill. My dream showed us getting evicted and it was so real that I remember feeling every emotion, so I literally jumped up out of my sleep with sweat on my forehead.

Once I got up, I started making phone calls and I got in touch with a social worker. I relayed to her my situation and she told me that she could place me and my son in a shelter right away. I asked her if the shelter had air conditioning and she told me it didn't. I let her know that I wouldn't be able to deal with the heat since I was pregnant. She said, "Think about what you want to do and if I can help in any way let me know."

The next couple of weeks, I kept trying to come up with a plan B for my living situation while simultaneously dealing with a complicated pregnancy due to my diabetes. I was at work when my manager came up to me and told me that I had a phone call, and my first thought was *it better not be my son again*. When I got to the phone, I heard Martha's voice. I asked her what she wanted. She then told me that the Sheriff's Department was at the apartment setting all of our belongings out on the street. I immediately went into shock and hung up. Then, I turned to my manager and told him I needed to leave because I had a family emergency. I quickly went to the locker room to change out of my uniform but I was shaking so bad I could hardly get dressed. One of my coworkers came in and helped me. All I could think about was *thank God I had that dream because now I have money to get storage space and a truck to move my mom's stuff off the street.*

As I was headed to the metro station I made a call to the social worker to let her know what was going down. She told me to call her as soon as I got to the closest metro station to the apartment. The social worker met me at the station, and we went to the storage place that I called. While I was on the way there, I paid for a truck too. Then, the social worker took me to the apartment and when we pulled up, my heart sank seeing all my mom's stuff on the sidewalk it was very painful.

The next phone call was to my pastor. When his wife answered, I told her what was going on and she said she would tell him as soon as he got home from work. She also told me that she would pick my son up from school and keep him at their house until we were finished which was a blessing. Later, my pastor called me and I asked him if he could help move my mom's stuff off the street and into my storage unit. He said he would make a phone call to find someone to help him then I told him I could not afford to pay him but I was willing to buy them some food.

I had an opportunity to talk to the Resident Manager of our building and she explained to me that my father had been issued many court summons to appear for non-payment of rent. That morning, she spoke to him to tell him if he brought her some of the money owed, she would hold off the eviction because she knew that when my mom was alive, the rent was always paid on time. While I was waiting for my friends to show up, my father pulled up with a small truck and I was so angry because of what the Resident Manager told me and I didn't want to speak to him. I kept asking myself *how could he let me leave the house without telling me what was about to go down within a couple of hours?!*

While my father was there, I did keep an eye on him to make sure he did not pick up any of my mom's furnishings. I made one last call to my uncle to see if my son and I could stay with them for a while until I came up with another solution and he told me to come over. The best thing that came out of this situation was that Chris no longer knew where I lived, so I didn't have to worry about him coming to bother me anymore. When I went back to work, I instructed everyone there not to give out any information about me to him.

Chapter 7

Losing Control

Aman from my past—Bob—would enter my life at one point (after my mom died), and this time it seemed like I had time to devote to someone. However, it would become apparent that we were looking for different things because I wanted to be in a committed relationship and he was looking for something casual. Basically just a sexual partner. I started to give him less time because that's not what I was interested in and as soon as he realized I was moving on with my life without him, he supposedly saw the light and was ready to commit.

When I look back and ask myself what attracted me to him I can't even tell you, but what I can say is that I was still stuck in a fragile state of mind. I still didn't understand my worth. So, I finally got what I wanted but he started to belittle my character by saying how I was with lots of other men before him and many other hurtful things to constantly tear me down verbally. I had to call on my inner strength and I started to turn it back on him. I was like, "Wait, you aren't an angel. I asked him, "Haven't you been with other women before me?" He said, "Yes, but that's different..." then he started to back off of me and my past.

He would get me so frustrated at him because he would promise me he was coming over and then he would not come but would call with plenty of excuses. I guess he didn't understand nor care that is an area that drives me crazy because when I was younger my father would always make me promises but would not follow through. It built up so much resentment.

Bob did some things that would get me so angry because I felt like he was playing games with my emotions. I used to visualize how I wanted to hurt him. I feel like since I kept so many emotional things bottled up inside, my temper would build up sometimes and I believe the only reason why I didn't act out on most of my thoughts was because I prayed a lot.

When I first started spending time talking with Bob, I thought he was so intelligent because he used big words and I was impressed. As the relationship began to get old and we settled in with each other, I started noticing some negative things. However, with a mindset that "I do not deserve any better," I made excuses for his behavior. I heard someone once say that when people show you who they are, believe them. If only I had heard this earlier.

When Bob told me one day that he was a difficult person to live with. I laughed it off as a joke but that was just one of several flags that I missed. One time, I was riding in the car with Bob and his mother. She came out and said to him, "Does she know about your mood swings?" as though I wasn't in the car with them. Again, the flag was waving and I laughed it off as a joke. Once, we were hanging out and he mentioned all nonchalantly that he used to drink a lot. I asked if it was still a problem but he quickly said it wasn't a problem anymore. The flag was waving again. It was near the holidays and my pastor was having a Christmas party and asked if I could bring someone. He said yes, so I told Bob about the invite but I noticed he was a little hesitant. Later, he got past it and we attended the party, but he seemed out of place. I just attributed it to not really knowing anybody there.

I then had a conversation with my pastor after the party so I asked him what his thoughts were about Bob. Because we are friends, he went to say how Bob seemed like a nice guy except for the fact he smelt alcohol on his breath. I was like, "No way, you are mistaken. Then he said, "I clearly am not mistaken I definitely smelled it on his breath." I was so shocked that he said that and I kept thinking about it and I was trying to remember if I noticed anything odd about that evening before we left for the party but sadly, I didn't.

I was trying to make some positive changes in my life so Bob and I had discussed joining a church together. It worked out that I ended up visiting a friend's church one Sunday and joined the same day. When I came home excited about my news, Bob wasn't happy and he even seemed mad. His excuse was "But we said we were going to do it together." I said, "Well when was that going to happen?"

Things started to get better for me after I made the decision to join the church. This was a confirmation to me. First, I got a great job offer and then I was able to purchase a car. But I started to notice a negative change in Bob's attitude toward me. It was almost as if he was jealous of the good things happening to me. The car was a major blessing for me because it meant that I no longer had to depend on him to take me places. It had become frustrating to be patient waiting on him—when he would tell me he was coming later, I would wait all day, then he would wait until evening, then say he'd come tomorrow instead.

I started to notice something else that I had a problem with; his attitude toward my son. It was always a little thing that he would try to make into a bigger issue and he would start an argument about it. That did not sit well with me because Emmanuel will always come first. Things were already beginning to feel uneasy between us when one evening my son came to me and told me he needed to talk to me about something. I could tell from his tone that it was serious so I said sure I asked him what it was. He proceeded to say, "Well, I talked to my teacher about how I should tell you this…" and at that moment, I felt horrible that my son felt like he couldn't come to me about anything. I was really nervous about what he was getting ready to say. My son told me that he was in our bathroom one night looking for something under the cabinet when he found liquor bottles under some towels and it looked like it had been hidden there. I was shocked at this news but tried not to show it to him. I thanked him for telling me and after he left my room, I took a deep breath while trying to get my thoughts together.

I called Bob into my room and he was like, "Yeah what's up?" I told him what my son just told me and he turned around real quick and said, "Where is he at?!" I grabbed him before he made it out of the room and I said, "You are not going to approach him and say anything to him because it took a lot for him to come to me so I know he is telling the truth." He was like, "I don't know what he is talking about." I looked him squarely in the eyes and said, "He does not have any reason to lie about it and I am going to say this only once: You best not bring any more alcohol into my house ever, if you want me in your future."

Immediately, I remembered what my pastor had said to me about smelling the alcohol on his breath. I thought to myself *he lied to me and I bet he does still have a drinking problem,* but I had been blind to the signs or he was hiding it really well. I made up my mind that I would start to pay attention more, so one time he came over and he fell asleep, I decided to check his overnight bag out of curiosity. Sure enough, I found a bottle of gin in there so I took it to the bathroom where I poured it out in the toilet. Then I set the bottle on the sink so he would see it.

Bob never said anything to me but I knew he was angry to see that I poured his alcohol out. He had enough sense not to bring it up to me since I told him, "Don't bring no more into my house." I didn't find any more alcohol coming into my house but I thought to myself *if it's a real problem then he might be doing the same thing at his house.* When we were over his mom's house I decided to check his bedroom and again I found bottles hidden in his drawers. Now I knew without a shadow of a doubt that he definitely still had a drinking problem. I waited until we got back to my house to confront him about what I found and I told him he needed to get some help. I also told him I would even go with him if he needed some support, but he said no and that he would go by himself.

Some weeks passed and I started to feel like he was working on his drinking problem. We were talking about secrets and he revealed to me that he was a part of some gang in the neighborhood and that he was asked to do some questionable things from time to time. However, when I tried to ask him more questions about it, he would only say he was not allowed to say any more than he already has. I was scared by his revelation to the point where I started to cry because I felt like I really did not know him. To make things worse, I had a suspicion that I was pregnant by him. As time passed I got confirmation that I was definitely pregnant again and I was nervous even though the father was in the picture. I had lots of questions about whether our relationship would make it through this pregnancy—my third child.

The stress of the pregnancy caused my diabetes to flare up again and things going on between us created extra stress that led to an increase in my blood sugar levels. My doctors decided to recommend that I be hospitalized in order to get my high glucose levels under control. Due to my necessary hospitalization, Bob had to be responsible for both Emmanuel and Miya which made me uneasy, but I did not have a better solution at the time.

Several days later I was back home, and I knew that my children weren't happy because they kept talking about Bob's lack of cooking skills. Bob started to tell me what I can and can't do once the baby comes. This made me so upset because with all my hormones, it just seemed like what he expected of me was going to be so overwhelming. Luckily, I talked to my godmother who told me, "Don't worry, about what he is saying all this now but when the baby comes, he will change his story," and that calmed me down.

One of the positive things was that his mom was excited about having another grandbaby on the way. The next months flew by and now it was time for the delivery. Thank God there were only a few hiccups but it all got worked out. Then my daughter was here. Nicole. Once I was released from the hospital, I had to plan how all of us were going to get along with everybody in my apartment. The first weeks were tough because Nicole had colic and we had to take turns just to get sleep because she would spend most of the night and way into the morning crying at the top of her lungs!

I was on maternity leave from my job and I had exhausted all of my leaves because I was so exhausted every morning from being up all night with my baby girl's crying. I knew I would not be in any condition to concentrate on my work while falling asleep. When I had exhausted all of my leaves, I had to prepare myself for the transition of going back to work and I was truly glad that baby girl was starting to get on a schedule of crying less at night. I don't remember exactly when it started but things just weren't the same in our relationship after the baby was born and I debated on when I was going to have a serious sit-down talk with Bob about how I was feeling. I felt like he needed to move back to his mother's house because I needed some space between us so that I could sort out my feelings for him but it took me a long time to get up the nerve to have that conversation.

———⁓◦◡◦◉◦◡◦⁓———

The health of Bob's mother wasn't good back then, and from time to time he would have to go back home to take care of her until she regained her strength unless his sister was there in his stead. It was the day after Christmas and Bob's mother again wasn't feeling well. He called me to tell me his mother wanted to know if I would come by the house to help her out and I told him of course I would so I got dressed then told the kids to get dressed since we were going over to Bob's mother's house for the day. When Bob arrived, we all went outside and got in the car and everything seemed good until in the middle of the ride I asked Bob some random question and he snapped at me. I looked at him sideways but I didn't respond. He started talking crazy and called me out by my name. I was like, "That's enough and don't talk to me like that while my kids are in the car." He kept mothing off so finally I said, "That's it. Take me back home right now." He replied, "No I won't. You are going to my house!"

I remember looking at my children's faces and they looked frightened, so I told myself to deescalate the situation by keeping calm until we got to his mother's house. I planned on calling a cab for me and my children so that we could go back home on our own. Unfortunately, my plan didn't work out as smoothly as I planned but I made a great attempt at an alternate escape plan. We all got out the car at his mom's house and I turned to my son and I said, "Take your baby sister and y'all go up the street to the 7-Eleven and wait for me." My poor son had a puzzled look on his face but he was ready to follow my orders.

As I went to put his baby sister in his arms Bob came towards me. Before I could get away, he had put both of his hands around my neck to choke me while my children were standing near. I could hear my son yelling at him to stop, then he finally eased up and he said, "My daughter isn't going nowhere" so he snatched her out my arms and headed into his mother's house. Emmanuel, Miya, and I followed him into the house. When we got in the house, I told Bob, "The children and I are leaving so hand the baby to me now," but he had a tight grip on her. He told me, "My mother is waiting on you," so I told him that I would go upstairs to tell his mother that I was sorry but I needed to go back home because I wasn't staying here with you.

I went and made some excuse for why I needed to leave, told his mom, then came back downstairs and told him to give me my baby because we were going back home. I looked at my son then I told him to go outside and wait for me. Then I called a cab and I pleaded with Bob to let me have my daughter. He was determined not to let her go. I heard my son call me to say that the cab had arrived so I told him to get in. I pulled and pulled at Bob's arms until he released his grip a little and I snatched our daughter from him while I ran to the cab. My head was spinning as I recalled all that happened with Bob because it felt like it was a horrible nightmare with a stranger, and I could not figure out what caused his weird behavior.

I did not know what to do or if I even wanted to see him again even though he is Nicole's father. *How am I supposed to deal with him now?!* I asked myself. I ended up setting up a meeting with my current Pastor to get some advice on what to do. I remember him saying, "I'm not going to tell you to leave because you may not be ready to do that, and I will not tell you to stay because that may not be safe. But I will advise you to pray that God will reveal some things to you so that you will get the answers you need to make a decision which is right for you."

One evening the children and I were watching television and having a great time when all of a sudden, the smoke detector started going off. Emmanuel and I checked everything out but there wasn't anything wrong. Then, it happened again. Emmanuel was like, "Let's just take the batteries out," but all I could see in my mind was the many news reports I had seen in the past when the fire investigators would say how a fire happened and the family had no working smoke detector so I told him to leave it alone. Several hours later, the kids and I were all asleep in our beds when the smoke detector went off again. All I could think about was *here we go again, another false alarm.* Even though I was really sleepy, I got up to check anyway. It was not a false alarm. All I saw were flames coming up from the carpet to the doorknob of the front door. I instinctively ran to the older children's room to warn them to get up and come into my room. When I got into my room I realized that my son never got up and his room was filling with smoke as he slept so I told my oldest daughter to go back to get him but she was like, "no way" so I went low crawled back and yelled for him to get up. When my son finally woke up, he stood straight up so I yelled, "It's a fire! Crawl to my room behind me." He did and we closed the door, put towels under the door, and then I called 911 to let them know exactly where we were located because since we were barricaded in my bedroom in the back and the other side of the building.

I was scared for us because the smoke was filling my room and I could feel the smoke burning my lungs. I told the dispatcher to hurry. It was a good thing my son had fire safety classes at his summer camp because he suggested pushing the screen out the window so the smoke could go out and we could get some fresh air inside the room where we were. I could hear the fireman trying to break through the front door, but it was too risky to bring us out that way. They brought a ladder to the side of the building where my bedroom was located. The fireman came up the ladder and said, "I'm going to bring each one of you down this way." My son made sure his sisters went first. When it was his turn he turned and looked back at me and said, "Mom, I love you." I told him, "I love you too, now get down that ladder!"

When the fireman came back to get me I was looking for my glasses and he said, "Come on we don't have time for that right now," so I stepped on the ladder with my bare feet. It was so hot and the fireman said, "I'm going to have to carry you." I said, "I know you been trained for this type of situation but if you drop me, I will never forgive you." The fireman got me down safely so that I could be reunited with my children but I was so surprised to see so many fire trucks, ambulances, and reporters.

Baby girl Nicole and I had to get some oxygen because we had inhaled so much smoke but while they were working on us, I overheard some conversations from people who had come out of their apartments to see what was going on. They were naming people who they believed may have set it.

The EMTs decided to transport baby girl and me to the hospital to get our oxygen levels up and someone had made a call to Bob to tell him what happened. While we were in the emergency room, I was visited by several men from the fire department. They started asking me questions, like: "Do you have any enemies, do you know of anyone who may have a grudge against you, and do you know of anyone who may have wanted to hurt you?" I told them that I had been complaining to management about some things but I felt that it wasn't anything that serious. Then I remembered what I heard the people talking about, so I mentioned to them that I heard people outside say that it may have been intentional. They replied that it was definitely purposely set. In other words, it was arson.

The gentlemen informed me that they were fire investigators trying to solve the mystery of what happened and why. After the investigators left, Bob arrived crying all on me and getting on my damn nerves. To make things worse, I smelled alcohol on his breath so I was like, "Pull yourself together because I been through enough tonight." As Bob was taking us to his mother's house, he was saying to the children that they would have to be quiet while they were at the house so they don't disturb his mother. In my head I was like *I just want to rest and just leave us alone because we just lived through a very traumatic ordeal that could have killed us.*

It was not as easy as I thought to get some sleep because every time I closed my eyes, it was like pushing rewind on a movie projector. My mind kept replaying the fire and everything else that happened over and over again. After a few days, I found out more of the details of what happened. Several stripers had moved into the building a couple of blocks down from mine. One of them had AIDS and gave it to this guy she was with. When he found out, he put out a hit on her and the guy set her building on fire with Molotov cocktails. This happened but was aimed at the wrong building and that's what caused the fire at our place. Everyone in my building was displaced but my apartment received the most damage.

We ended up staying at Bob's mother's house until the apartment complex fixed up another apartment for us. The best thing that happened to me while we were waiting was my pastor called to check on us when he got word about what happened. He asked what we needed and I named some things we needed and he made sure that the church members donated the items. I will never forget my first church service after the fire. I tore that carpet up thanking and praising God for bringing me and my family through the fire.

The investigators never did find the guy they suspected of setting the fire. When we were able to move into the other apartment, I finally had that serious talk with Bob and I got straight to the point. I let him know that I needed some space. Then I told him that he needed to stop spending nights at my apartment too. He started coming up with his own compromises regarding the situation since it was obvious that I no longer wanted to be intimate with him. He offered to stay the night but only sleep on the floor instead of being in bed next to me. His reasoning was that he just wanted to be around to spend time with his daughter. I felt bad and I agreed to go along with his suggestion for the sake of our daughter.

When I started to think about how long I had been feeling like the intimacy was lost, I realized that it started during the middle of my pregnancy with Nicole. All I remember was that one day, Bob went to touch me in an intimate way but I felt physically sick to the point I thought that I would throw up. That was the beginning of many times of becoming ill whenever he wanted to be intimate. He eventually stopped trying to try to have sex with me while I was pregnant.

The compromise I agreed to was short lived because one day, we were just hanging out in my room and he climbed into my bed and tried to touch me in a sexual manner. I started swinging my arms in his direction then I yelled, "See now you have to get out!" He had the nerve to look at me in shock so I repeated what I said. Then I said, "Pack your stuff and leave!"

I did agree that he could come over when he wanted to see his daughter (within reason) if he gave me advance notice. One day, I was out and ran into this guy and I gave him my number since in my mind *I'm single again*. Later, I realized that I needed to establish some ground rules with Bob when he'd come over to my house because in his mind he still lived at my house. His actions whenever he visited were to take over the house. So when he came over, I let him know that when he comes over don't take it upon himself to answer or open my door, and by all means do not answer my phone. He agreed to my terms.

The next day that Bob came over, I was in my bedroom and I heard my house phone ringing. Then it stopped. I went into the kitchen to see Bob hanging up the phone. I felt my anger building up but I tried to contain it as I went into kitchen because the children were around. I said, "Did I hear the phone ring?" Bob replied by saying, "Yeah, some guy called and asked to speak to you." I walked away and waited in my room until I heard Bob was about to leave. I followed him out and said to him, "We need to talk about what just happened in the house." He looked at me puzzled. When we got outside to the parking lot, I asked him, "Do you remember the conversation we had about how you are supposed to act when you're at my apartment?" He said yes. I said, "What possessed you to answer my phone?" He gave me that dumb look again. The next thing he said was, "So you are talking to someone else now…" I said, "We are friends who talk on the phone." Bob was about to leave so I said, "Oh by the way, do not pick up Nicole today from the daycare because I am picking her up." He agreed.

After I got off work I headed to the daycare center to pick up Nicole. When I got inside, they told me Nicole was gone and that her father already picked her up. The whole way home, I was practicing what and how I was going to say what I needed to say to Bob. When I get to the house, then he had the nerve to answer my door like he still lived there! Again he was saved by the children being around so I had to hold my tongue, but on the inside I was furious!

Bob was acting like everything was normal and he had the nerve to tell me, "I'm cooking dinner and it will be ready soon." I mumbled loud enough for only him to hear, "Didn't I tell you not to pick up Nicole today?" He tried to give me some lame excuse but I was too mad to hear anything he had to say. I headed straight for my room to change out of my work clothes and to calm down for the sake of the children not getting caught up in our argument. I really needed to say some things to him in detail about our failing relationship, but it was not the time nor the place for that conversation.

While I was in my room waiting for Bob to finish cooking dinner, I had time to calm down and plan what my next move was going to be because the older children had grown attached to him. It wasn't going to be easy to make a clean break from him. After a few minutes, Bob came into the room and brought me my dinner with a big smile on his face—as though he had not totally disregarded my wishes earlier.

I started to eat my dinner while Bob was going on and on about me and him. For most of the conversation, I was tuning him out. Then I started to notice that he was pacing back and forth and his tone started to sound erratic. He was rambling on and at some point, I started to feel a negative energy fill the room. I started to fear him for a moment. In my head, I told myself *if tries anything crazy I'm going to hit him with this plate.* He asked me something again about the guy that had called the house and I said, "Look leave me alone while I'm eating my dinner." The next thing I knew, he was trying to grab me by the neck and I swung my plate at him out of reflex. He punched me in my face and I moved out of his path because he looked like he was about to do more so I said I was calling the police. I then noticed he was bleeding and he said, "Go ahead and call them because you will be the one going to jail as soon as they see my injuries."

Our daughter was in the room while this was going on and he leaned over her and said, "Look at what your mother did to me." I wasn't taking any chances on trusting him so I dialed 911 then I called my godmother and told her what happened. I told her that if they arrested me I needed her to come get my children. When the police arrived, I saw the questioning look on my son's face like *what happened,* but I told my son to take his sisters to their room while I talked to the police. One officer took Bob aside and the other was questioning me about my version of what happened. While the officer was talking to me he asked me who had custody of my daughter and I said she lives with me so of course I do. Then he asked me if it was established in the courts. I asked him what he meant by that and he replied, "You need to go to the courthouse to get paternity legally as soon as possible before he does." Then the other officer came out of the bedroom with Bob and they mentioned Bob's obvious injury. They asked him if he wanted to press charges against me. I kept my head down as I heard him say yes. I lifted up my head to ask if I could call a family friend to come get my kids. Bob had a change of heart after hearing that so the cop who had been talking to him earlier said, "Just to let you know, you have up to a year to change your mind if you want to press charges."

The officers then left and took Bob with them so he could get checked to see if he would need stitches for his forehead after the plate I swung at him cut him. After the police left, I opened the door to the bedroom where the children were so I could have a talk with them because I wanted them to know that everything was going to be okay and that Bob wouldn't be coming around anymore.

Chapter 8

Family Betrayal

My cousin Lizzie suggested we go out one night, I asked her where because we didn't have a babysitter and then she said we can drop the kids off at her house so my uncle would watch all the kids while we went out. She had a male friend who had a friend that wanted to meet a woman so they put us on the phone together for a few minutes. Then he invited my cousin and me over to his apartment for a boxing match viewing party. When we walked in, some girls were walking out but before they left, they looked my cousin and me up and down, giving us a nasty look. Lizzie and I ended up being the only women left and several guys were there drinking and watching the fight.

Since I didn't know any of the guys, I just stood there looking around while my cousin went searching for the guy she knew. The guy who lived in the apartment who I spoke to on the phone before coming over came up to introduce himself to me as Larry. He told me to have a seat then he sat catty-corner to me and we talked for a long time as though we were old friends. We laughed a lot. Some of the guys there tried to distract him from our conversation, but he just waved them off and continued to focus on me. Some female neighbor showed up and tried to talk to him but he brushed her off as well and I saw the look on her face—she was totally pissed off that he was ignoring her. I was like, "It's okay if you need to talk to her, I don't mind." He was like, "She's not important…" Then, my cousin announced she's ready to leave. I turned to him to say that I had to leave even though I wasn't ready to because I was enjoying the conversation and his company.

He pleaded with me to stay and let her go but I felt really uncomfortable because I would be the only female there when she left and I didn't know anyone there either so she kept looking at me like *come on let's go…* I ended up staying. It was the beginning of a whirlwind romance that I never saw coming and I never expected to fall for him because he was much younger than me. I felt like we were soulmates. We could almost read each other's minds. Our birthdays were 6 days apart and he included my children in the picture as well. I also developed a relationship with his children.

One day, my cousin and I decided to call up my friend Larry and see what plans he had for Memorial Day celebration. He said he had invited some friends over so we suggested that we go to the store and get some food to cook for everybody. He agreed that that was a great idea. When we arrived at the house, he greeted me with a hug and kiss then we proceeded to the kitchen. I was so excited to celebrate the holiday with everyone. The music was on and everybody was coming in and out. Lots of laughter and drinks being passed around. In the middle of the party, Larry wanted to slip off for some intimate time. I loved the spontaneity of our relationship. He asked my cousin to cover for us if anyone noticed us missing.

Finally, the food was ready and the whole night, Larry kept flirting and complementing me in front of everyone. My cousin's friend arrived drunk and caused a big scene, so Larry put him out. As the day party turned to a night party Larry surprised me by putting on some slow music and grabbing me up in his arms in front of everybody telling me to dance with him. I tried to pull away because I was shy but the look he gave me when he asked me again melted my heart, so we danced. When we finished, I looked around at everybody clapping. Then I looked at my cousin and I saw a really strange look on her face as she made a negative comment about us. Immediately, I recognized that look as jealousy and Larry picked up on it too. He told her, "Don't worry. Someday, you will find someone to love you like this."

After that interaction, I realized that I had to stop inviting her to events we had and stop telling her so much about our relationship matters. I followed through on my plan to cut back on including Lizzie in my relationship progress but I started to notice another pattern developing. Every time I would talk to her, she would mention to me that she had a conversation with Larry. At that point, I realized that I should have a conversation with Larry about my concerns about the boundaries she seemed to be crossing in our relationship.

I didn't think clearly enough about my approach when I presented my concerns to him. I was explaining it to him through the eyes of a woman and he quickly said, "No way, there's nothing to this." So I left it alone. I tried my best not to admit that I had my intuition eating at me because it seemed as though she was having separate conversations with him every day. Finally, I felt I had to come to her woman to woman and ask her point blank, "Lizzie is there something going on between Larry and you that I should know about?" Her response was "No way, we're just friends." With that, I left it alone because at the end of the day, she is family, we were tight, and she would never do that to blood.

My wonderful world would begin to unravel when I was spending some peaceful alone time with Larry. He mentioned to me that he had a court case coming up and I listened but brushed it off because I was too caught up in our moment. Several days later, he brought it up again and this time, I paid attention enough to ask some questions. The answers put me at ease, so I left it alone. I had almost forgotten that I received a letter from the courthouse telling me that I had been selected for jury duty coming up, so I was preparing for the call-in day. The next thing I knew, Larry was telling me that a court date has been set and it was official but I picked up on a different tone as he talked about it that time.

I felt nervous and I wanted to know more. He laid out all his options and the consequences he's up against. Then I went silent trying to absorb this because I knew that this happened before I knew him, I will support him through it. I asked him what the date was so I can be there for him. My heart dropped when he said the date because it was the same day I was scheduled for jury duty. If it had been anything else I could get it rescheduled. But with jury duty, if it isn't death or hospitalization, you're not getting out of it (which I learned from past experience)!

We made it our goal to spend as much time as we could with each other including spending time with the children for the week leading up to the impending court date. Getting ready that morning was hard, and Larry called me before I left for jury duty. I wished him luck in court, and we promised to call each other later. It was basically a sit-and-wait situation for me at the courthouse. While waiting in the jury room, we were able to watch movies or have snacks and beverages from the vending machines. The whole time though, my mind was on Larry. Just as they were about to call names of people selected for the next jury my cellphone rang. I looked down and it was Larry but I couldn't talk anymore so I turned the ringer off. I thought to myself: *I will call him back* and I would regret that decision for the longest of time.

I was glad that I had officially completed my civic duty by appearing and making myself available by being on-call but I was not chosen to be on a jury and was free to leave. I couldn't wait to leave the courthouse grounds so I could call and check on my man! I called his phone several times and he never responded. Finally, I called his best friend and roommate and I said I've been trying to get in touch with Larry and he wasn't answering his phone. I asked if he was in the house yet. His best friend lowered the bombshell on me and said Larry's mom called me to say they took him in to custody. They locked him up. I remember I was at the gas station getting ready to pump gas and I think I stopped breathing because I was so stunned. I fumbled with the words to say next and I had so many questions with no answers and my head was spinning. I was like, "How can I talk to him?" All he could say was "I guess you have to wait until he contacts you."

I shed so many tears after I got the news and I just kept replaying the whole day over and over again in my mind and telling myself *if only I had just stepped out of the jury room and took that call.* All of a sudden, I had no idea if I will hear from or see him again. I didn't know any specific details. I was in so much pain and it felt like someone had just ripped my heart out of my chest. When I was finally able to stop crying my eyes out, I decided to call my cousin and tell her the news. I took a deep breath to get myself together so that I wouldn't break down in tears while I spoke to her. As I poured my heart out to her, at some point I noticed she was shockingly quiet. When I finished and I took another deep breath, I said, "I can't believe this has happened." She replied, "I can!"

This day sent me through so many emotional roller coasters and now the only family that I felt close to just sent the most icy vibes through the phone. Once I caught what she said, I was like, "What do you mean?" She proceeded to keep this cold tone with me saying, "He got what he deserves and so what anyway?" I was like, "What, why are you talking about him like that, I thought he was your friend and now we do not know long he will be locked up. I called you thinking you would understand how much I am going through right now and your being downright mean." She told me, "Why do you care anyway?" I said, "Because I'm in love with him (regretting now that I never told him)." She replied, "Please, you have said that before." I said, "I really mean it but I don't have to prove anything to you," and I hung up the phone!

The next weeks were almost unbearable. Not hearing from him and no news of what was going on with him. It had even started to affect my ability to perform at my job because every time I would think of him I would start to cry and my heart would hurt so bad. I have never experienced any feelings or emotions like this about any man. I had confided in a co-worker about all the loss and pain I was experiencing and they suggested I pour all of my pain into a letter. I did it and it did help. So many pages were soaked with tears.

One day, I was at work and I received a collect call and it said it was coming from a correctional facility. I heard his voice when he said his name and my goodness, you would have thought I won an award! I was so excited! I searched around the office for an empty room so I could talk to him in private and shed all the happy tears I felt welling up inside! Whew, what a relief to finally hear his voice. He sounded so good and I was talking so fast trying to get answers to all my questions in the short amount of time I had to talk to him. One of my biggest questions how much time and he said the maximum could be 18 months—could be less—depending on circumstances.

All of this terminology was foreign to me. I asked why it took him so long to get in touch with and he said he didn't have access to his phone so he had been in touch with the guy he used to work with who knew my cousin and got her number to ask for my number, but she kept telling him she had to look for it and he said he had to keep asking her and after a long time, she finally found the number. I refused to waste our precious time to discuss my cousin Lizzie but I had not spoken another word to her since she acted funny towards me when I called her about Larry getting locked up. Then I discovered she purposely tried to withhold my phone number from him.

My children wanted to have contact with their cousins—Lizzie's children—so I took my children over to her house so they could spend time together. She acted like she couldn't speak to me even to say hi, so I just dropped off my kids and left because I sure wasn't going to beg her to speak to me. Larry's phone calls were coming more frequently now and I felt a little better about the situation but I was still missing him terribly. During one of our phone calls, Larry told me he may have some good news to give me soon and I was like, "Don't tease me, what is it?" He told me he applied for work release and that it could mean he could be able to see me because the job he applied for was near my house. I was anxiously excited. I was trying not to get my hopes up just in case it all fell through, but the Lord knew I was missing me some of him! I did not want to keep asking about it so I just kept praying that he would be approved and I knew he would share the good news with me when it came.

Larry called me one evening and asked me the usual—how was my day, and then he asked what my plans for tomorrow were... I mentioned that I was probably going to take off to take care of some business. We ended our conversation as usual with "love you and good night."

The next day, I was cleaning up in my apartment before leaving to take care of my business. My phone rang and I almost didn't answer because I didn't recognize the number but I did answer it and I heard Larry's voice saying, "Come to the door and let me in." I couldn't get to that door fast enough to put my arms around his neck and give him the most passionate kiss ever! Needless to say I never made it out the house to take care of my business because my first priority was getting reacquainted with my man. After we took a breath, I said, "Why didn't you tell me you were coming?" He said, smiling, "I wanted to surprise you."

He gave me a permanent grin on my face again and several times during the week he would see me either before or after work. Some special days, I would see him twice a day. A month later, something strange happened and I stopped hearing from him and I didn't know how to get in touch with him to find out what was going on. He got in touch with me after a little more than a month and he said someone had broken into his car and stole his cellphone so he couldn't get back and forth to work until he found another means of transportation.

Larry called me several days later to ask me if he can make arrangements to authorize me to come up to the correctional facility so I would be able to come pick him up for work in the mornings. I was like, "It depends on what time I would have to be there and where would I have to come too." He said he'd get back to me after all the arrangements were made. Arrangements were finalized after about a week, and I was on my way to picking him up for work. It got easier to do once I got the route memorized. I so enjoyed our times together even if it were not exactly how I would have wanted it to be.

Larry got his car fixed so I didn't have to come pick him up anymore and everything seemed to be going good again. Then another stumbling block came when the calls stopped again and there were no more visits. This time around, I started making phone calls. I finally got word that there had been a riot at the jail and so they stopped all phone calls, visitations, and work release but no one knew for how long. It was a wait-and-see thing with everybody on standby to see when this would be over.

———∿∿∾∾⊙⊀⊙⊀⊙∾∾∿∿———

It was the first day of the girls' spring break so I was able to get to work early because I did not have to catch a bus to the babysitter's house. I talked to my supervisor about coming in early for that week because the kids were out on break. I was in the middle of doing some work and I had started to walk away from my desk when the phone rang, and it was my cousin Lizzie. Lizzie proceeded to question me about a conversation that I had with her sister previously and I recalled running into her sister at the metro station. She had mentioned to me that her sister Lizzie was pregnant and I was surprised because she never mentioned it to me even though we were no longer close as we once were. I said I do remember the conversation we had and then Lizzie said, "I hear you have been asking questions about my baby's father and I told her, "I don't even know who the father is." That was when she (stabbed me in my heart) and said, "Larry is the father of my baby!"

She then told me that anything that I say to her sister will be repeated to her and I told her I did not care if it was repeated to her. I then asked her, "If Lizzie wanted to be with Larry, why did she introduce me to him in the first place?" Lizzie said she didn't want him and then she said all those times when I asked her if anything was going on between them they had not been together. Lizzie then told me it happened just before he got locked up.

When she told me that, my mind then went back to the day I called her upset when I got word that day Larry went to court and he ended up getting locked up and I didn't answer his last call to me because I figured I would talk/see him later because I had jury duty that day. I remember talking to her about how heartbroken I was because I realized how much I loved him and she was so cold towards me that I decided to cut her back after she told me, "Oh yeah, you're always saying you are in love with someone."

I then asked where the baby came from. And she said, "We had sex but he had your car," and then she pushed the knife into my heart even deeper by saying, "He was just using you," and before I was about to explode, I asked her why she didn't tell me all of this before. She replied that she told him to be honest with me about how he didn't want to be with me. She then told me that she wrote him a letter 2 months before the baby was born to tell him he was the father of the baby she was about to have. I was truly stunned and to top it all off she told me, "You can just pretend that we aren't related." I told her she didn't have to worry about that because it's not a problem because I wish we weren't related and I said, "No wonder you didn't want to speak to me." She replied, "No. It's because you are so self-righteous!"

When I hung up the phone I had to go vent. I spoke to a co-worker and then I went into the restroom to get a good cry out. Then I got myself together. After that, I went through every emotion there is during the grief process because that was how I felt. Just like someone died and I felt like I was dying inside too. Lizzie's words just kept swirling around in my head over and over. Eventually, I built up so much anger towards Lizzie first because she is family, then Larry if everything that she said was true and a baby was now on the way!

The hurt and anger were getting so bad that I was going to bed dreaming about running them over, and Lord I hate to say it, but it felt so good. When I thought back about the time I was first introduced to Larry, I believe my cousin never imagined that Larry and I would end up liking each other. But when she saw the feelings we had developed for each other, she decided to plan to do whatever it took to break us up because her relationships weren't working out. I was spending more time with Larry and keeping her out the loop so she was jealous.

Several weeks passed and I was sleeping so good when the phone rang and I heard this male voice on the other end of the line saying, "Wake up." I mumbled, "why?" Then the voice said, "get up," and then I realize it wasn't my son so I slightly started to wake up and I ask, "Who is this?" The male voice said, "it's your husband." I was starting to wake up and I figured out who the voice belonged to based on his laugh. I then knew it was Larry so I quickly blurted out, "You got a lot of nerve calling me!" He asked why, so I said, "I know all about Lizzie and the baby!" He said, "I don't believe that it's my baby."

I told him all about the conversation we had when she called me at work to tell me that he was the father of her baby. He asked about my car being under a protective car cover and I told him yes it was then he told me he had to call Lizzie twice before she finally gave him my number. He asked if he could come over. I hesitated. He said, "Don't tell me you don't love me" (if only he knew how much I really did) and the weak me gave in and let him come over.

Larry called me back to ask if the girls were up and I said they were still asleep so he told me he was on the way over. His body was in great shape and all that exercise while he was locked up did his body lots of good, but he shaved off all his hair. I could not believe he had the nerve to ask me if I had been seeing anyone. I told him yes. He told me to get rid of him now that he was back in the picture. He also asked if I had been intimate with the guy and I told him that I had been good while he was gone. He asked me to prove it. It had been so long since we had been intimate, and it was not as good as it had been in the past, but I did not mind because I was glad to be near him again.

He kissed me goodbye and all the old feelings were flooding back and I knew that I needed to cut the other guy out of my life as soon as possible. I was really glad that the relationship never went to the next level. Lizzie is my cousin but I really believed Larry when he said the baby wasn't his because I asked myself *why did she wait so long to tell Larry that she was pregnant by him if it's really his baby* and *he wasn't just using me because I haven't even been in the picture.*

Another thing I thought about was how several years before, there was a question about one of her children's paternity and she went all the way to court to confirm paternity only to find out the guy she accused of being her child's father turned out not to be the father after she had talked bad about him to all the family. She was so embarrassed that she kept saying it must be a mistake. I guess we should have told her that DNA tests do not lie. Lizzie had four kids before this pregnancy and none of the kids' fathers paid her child support. Larry was a good father who always took care of his kids and I believe that's why my cousin wanted to put her baby on him.

Larry was released early on probation but he had to wear an ankle bracelet and he had a curfew for work too. When he got released, he moved in with his youngest son's mother but he had led me to believe he was staying with his mom. I found out by accident though because I noticed that he kept calling me from an unfamiliar number. I wanted to ask him something and I called him back on the number but a woman answered. I was so surprised that I just held the phone then hung up. The girl obviously caught on that it was strange that someone would just hang up and he was trying to come up with a quick lie so I figured out that she must have told him to call back so she could find out who I was.

My head was spinning trying to figure out what was going on and then my phone rang and I could hear him saying, "I don't even know whose number it is." In other words, he was telling me to play along with the lie and I did help him out and I told her I didn't know who he was. When I hung up, I was so furious that I was shaking and instead of calling me back to explain, he came to my house days later. He brought his best friend over with him because he knew his friend and I got along good. I guess he figured it would soften the blow.

He put his friend up to talking to me first and after I told his friend that Larry really messed up with me, his friend was like, "Yeah he knows he messed up." He was just standing there all quiet, looking sad, and then he tried to hug me but I pulled away. I told his friend, "Maybe I will forgive him after he explains to me why he lied to me but right now I'm not ready to forgive him." They turned to leave and when his friend got out the door he turned back to me and hugged me and said, "I'm sorry" then left.

Of course I would forgive him and he knew that but he said he figured that I would be mad if he told me he was staying with his son's mother. I said, "If it's just a place to stay but you aren't rekindling a relationship with her then I don't have a problem with it." The situation between them did end up getting tense and so he did end up having to go stay with his parents, but it was very inconvenient especially with limited transportation and the place being far away from his job. We were on the phone one night venting about different things we were dealing with and we came up with the great idea that we should move in together. Oh well it seemed like a great idea when we first talked about it, but it was not as wonderful as we thought it was going to be for both of us. He had to have all these things before he moved in and one of the main things was a separate telephone line, so his ankle bracelet monitoring system could be hooked up. And he wanted cable.

———— ·ᴡᴡ·ᴏ·ᴏ·ᴏ·ᴏ·ᴏ·ᴡᴡ· ————

While we were living together, my cousin Lizzie contacted Larry and even went to the extreme of bringing the baby to his job then he said the baby does not look anything like me but exactly just like her. Once we got used to living with each other, things were okay between us and then I would get word that my uncle had passed away (Lizzie's dad). Because of that, I had to prepare to see my cousin after all the bad blood between us. I was willing to do that though, to pay my respects to my uncle and say my final goodbye to him because my uncle was good to me and my children.

The day of the funeral started off rough and I remember Larry having a talk with me saying, "You and your cousin need to squash the beef between each other. If not for each other's sake then do it for your uncle." At that moment, he was so right. I told myself even though I felt like I didn't do anything wrong, I would be the better person today in honor of my uncle. The children and I arrived a little late, so we had to sit several rows back on the family side, but I did spot my cousin Lizzie in the front row. At some point during the funeral, my cousin stood up to go to the bathroom and once she spotted me she, purposely went the long way around the church to avoid me. I tried to tell myself that it wasn't really like that.

That was the first time I saw the baby that she claimed was Larry's child and all I see is that he looks just like her. My thoughts that she was ignoring me were later confirmed when we were at the repast. She went out of her way to talk to my children who were standing next to me but didn't even crack her lips even to say hello. I did go to her sisters and gave them my number. I asked them to give her my number and said, "Can you tell your sister to call me please," but that phone call never came. I made up in my mind that I had tried, and she did not want to talk to me so I refused to beg her and so I was done with it!

———∽∽•◦◦◦∿∿•∿∿∽∽∞————

Larry and I started having financial problems because I thought he was going to be helping with the bills but I didn't calculate that he was paying child support for three children... and then there were his probation fees. If they weren't paid, he was at risk of having to go back to jail to serve the rest of his time out. Then, I noticed there were other females calling the house for him that were not the mother of his children. When I would question him about it, he would say they're just friends. It became incredibly stressful when the bills started piling up and we were fussing and arguing more and more.

One time, Larry had to go to court because the monitoring system wasn't giving out a good signal so they were going to determine what was going to happen. I kept asking him, "If they say you have to move, where will you go? He said he didn't know, so I said, "I will go to court with you." He said, "No you don't have to do that."

He came back from court and he said, "They say I have to move again." I asked where he was going but he wouldn't tell me. I didn't want to believe it but I found out that he went back to his youngest son's mother's house because she took ill and had to be hospitalized. He had to take care of his son and stepdaughter. Once his son's mother got well, they could not get along again, and he had to move back to his parents' house. We kept in touch on and off for years, but it would not be the same especially when I found out that he married his oldest son's mother.

We did rekindle the fire just once or twice years later. We were both invited to a birthday party for a mutual friend and believe me I went out of my way to look my best when I found out he was coming. I went with a good girl friend and we got there somewhat early so when he arrived much later, I played like I did not even notice him. He came up to me to say hello. While I was on the dance floor with my friends, I had too much to drink and I was showing off and making sure he saw me. Then I fell on my butt—I was truly hoped he didn't see that part.

We were leaving the party around the same time and he tried to speak to me, but I was still playing hard to get so we said our goodbyes. When I was driving my best friend home, he called me to say how good it was to see me. He mentioned how he noticed that I fell on the dance floor and we both laughed. I told him that I was dropping my friend off at her house and then he asked what was I doing after that. I said I was going home. He asked me to come by his old roommate's apartment. I said I'll think about it and call him back.

So, I thought about how good it was to see him and I missed him, so I called him to tell him I was on the way. It was really nice to see both of the guys and it was the first time I met his best friend's girlfriend. We had drinks and lots of laughs then I caught him giving his friend some kind of signal to leave us alone. We talked about old times and he complimented me on how good I looked. Then he said you did not look this good when we were together, so I laughed. The next thing I knew, we were kissing and he was caressing me, and all those old feelings came flooding back. He asked me to stay the night but I looked around like, "What, in the living room?" He went and asked his friend if we could spend the night and he asked the girlfriend if it was okay. She said we could sleep in the kids' room. We didn't do much sleeping and when we were about to leave the next morning we had smiles on our faces. His best friend's girlfriend said, "I hope you know the walls in here are very thin." He laughed, but I was embarrassed when I remembered all we did all night and into the morning.

Chapter 9

African Chameleon

Nicole moved in with Emmanuel so she could stay in her same high school and graduate without having to readjust to a new school for graduation. I was finally ready to move on to an independent journey and after much searching, I found a room in the Annapolis, Maryland area. I had an interview with this African lady who was renting a room in her home. She explained that her husband is in the Navy and had been deployed so she needed some help covering the household bills. The amount she was asking for was a little higher than I had budgeted for, but it was convenient, and I had a timeframe that I wanted to be moved out by. She took me around for a little tour of the house and it was alright. Not as clean as I would like but most of the time I will be at work or in my room anyway. She also introduced me to the couple who was renting the room downstairs and they seemed to be nice.

When I told friends and family that was about to move in with an African woman, I got lots of negative feedback, but I brushed it off. The way my situation was going, I had no other choice but to pray and make this move until I could do better. I was able to get my stuff moved in between working my shifts. It didn't take long before the negative things started happening. and it started one night when I came home late after working a long shift. I went into the kitchen, flipped on the light and I saw one million roaches everywhere—even on the ceiling—so I had to jump back out of the kitchen so they would not fall in my hair! I forgot why I went in there and lost any appetite I may have had.

Several days later, I was in my room when I smelled this awful aroma filling my room's air so I opened up my door and started to go downstairs only to discover it was coming from the kitchen. It was Bintu cooking her African food. It smelled so bad, so I went back to my room and opened my window to try to let some of that funk out. It didn't help much so I left out earlier than planned so that smell would not get in my work clothes. The next week, I heard a male voice coming from the bathroom so finally I asked Bintu about the guy I saw and heard upstairs. She told me that it was her brother. I was really puzzled because she never mentioned to me that her brother was staying there, and I felt a little uneasy since he was in the bedroom across mine.

One day, I was in my room and I heard a knock on my door. I hesitated before I opened the door. I asked myself *who could be knocking on my door*? I opened it to see Bintu's brother smiling at me. I just looked at him and I said, "How can I help you?" He introduced himself and he was asking me stuff… I was ready to cut the conversation and close my door so I made an excuse by saying I needed to get ready for work. Bintu's brother was getting on my nerves because he would go in the bathroom early in the morning having loud conversations. I thought he was on his cellphone only to find out from the couple downstairs he was talking to himself because he has some mental issues. That's why he hadn't been living there the whole time because his sister had him living somewhere else for a while.

Several days later, her brother would knock on my door again, grinning. He reached out his hand with a little box and he opened it up so I could see a ring inside. He said it's for me to be his friend. I quickly said, "Oh no, I can't accept it because I have a boyfriend." He got mad and I quickly shut the door. Wow that went weirdly creepy, and I knew I was going to have to have a talk with Bintu right away because it was looking like I was going to have a problem with him. I got to talk to Bintu about her brother and she said she would definitely talk to him about crossing my boundaries.

After that, I tried to avoid him at all costs but it was bound to happen that we would run into each other in the house. I was in the kitchen when he came downstairs. He opened the refrigerator, looked in it, and started grinning at me. Another day, I was relaxing in my room when I heard a loud commotion in the hallway. I opened my bedroom door to see Bintu and her brother going at it, fussing in their language. I just closed my door so they could continue their little dispute amongst themselves. Then all of a sudden, I heard an even bigger commotion like someone had fallen. I jumped up and opened my door again to see that Bintu had pushed the mattress from the bedroom that her brother was staying in down the stairs. It looked as though it was almost on top of him. I stood there looking and my mouth was wide open as I stood there in shock. I quickly went back to my room because the look on her brother's face said he wanted to hurt her.

I moved to get dressed as fast as I could to leave early because I did not want to be in the house with all that chaos going on. As I was headed to the door and towards my car, I saw the police were at the bottom of the steps questioning Bintu about what was going on. I was a little nervous about what to expect when I got home that night after I worked my shift, but thank goodness it was quiet, so it was at least a peaceful night.

Most days I worked long hours during the holidays but then my hours were being reduced so I was at home more and I started to notice that the kitchen was not clear. When I took a look around, I also noticed that when Bintu cooked, she would leave a big mess. One day the lady that lived downstairs started talking about taking turns to keep the kitchen clean. We also discussed putting together to get food for meals to cook since we both agreed we didn't want anything that Bintu was cooking since we saw how she was unclean in food prep before and after.

Bintu also owned a little dog that in the beginning didn't pose a problem for me but something changed. First, I would notice pee puddles throughout the house. She put up a gate to seclude the dog to only one section of the house but then her dog would start to cry and whine all hours of the early morning to the point that I started recording how bad it was getting so that I would take my complaints to Bintu before leaving the house. The next thing I started noticing was that when I came down to the kitchen in the morning, I saw a trail of dog poop and I nearly stepped on it. I was like *how many issues do I have to deal with in this house?* Of course that led to another conversation with Bintu.

The lady that lived in the basement came upstairs while I was in the kitchen one time, and I asked her if Bintu's brother was contributing to the food in the house. She told me he didn't, and I was so mad about that but I was never able to confirm if he was touching my food.

Several months down the road, I had walked into the kitchen after working a long shift so I was greeted by the woman from downstairs who informed me that Bintu wanted to have some kind of emergency house meeting. I looked at her and said, "Not tonight because I am exhausted." All I want to do was go to my room and relax so I proceeded upstairs to my room. While I was in my room getting undressed, there was a knock on my door and it was the lady from the basement who said, "Bintu told me to tell you it is important that you come downstairs so she can talk to us." I snapped and said I'd be down in a little while and at that point, I was truly pissed off!

When I came down into the kitchen, they had some chairs set up so we can listen to Bintu talk. I sat down and crossed my arms in defiance for the mess that was about to go down. So Bintu began speaking to us with her broken English which I could hardly understand. Basically she said that the electric bill came in and it was extremely high so she wanted us to contribute more money to her to cover the bill. I was furious because this woman must think I am stupid. I know my rights, so I said out loud, "Wait a minute, the ad you posted for my room said everything was included. You expect each one of us to pay this extra amount? What about your brother, is he also paying? When I signed my lease nowhere on there does it say anything about the electricity bill being a separate bill. It was to be included in my rent amount." I stood up and said, "I will not be giving up any of my hard-earned money to help with this bill." I walked right back upstairs.

I laid on my bed replaying what just happened downstairs and the fact that she tried to intimidate me by saying I had to help pay that bill truly fired me up every time I thought about it. I realized she was in the club with several other people who have underestimated me. They thought that because I'm nice they can take my niceness for weakness, but in this instance, I am smart enough to know my tenants' rights and what I don't know, I can research and find out.

The next day when I got home, I went downstairs to talk to the couple who were renting the basement to get a feel about how they felt about the meeting. I quickly realized that I was going to be on my own with this fight because they were all intimidated by this woman. They just kept saying if we don't pay she going to put us out. I was like, "Pull your lease agreement out because I want to show you something." The woman reluctantly pulled it out and gave it to me. I said, "Just as I thought." I pointed to the wording of the contract where it stated the amount of rent she expected but it did not say anything about them paying a separate amount for the electricity. They were so scared they couldn't get my point that Bintu had no legal grounds to evict them for something she never included in their lease!

After speaking to them, I went back upstairs to my room to regroup mentally to formulate a plan against this woman who obviously felt like she can change the house rules whenever she wanted it to work in her favor. She crossed paths with the wrong person. I was about to show her I could call her bluff. After thinking about it, I felt like something didn't smell right about the whole situation and needed to get to the bottom of what was really going on. I was going to play into her situation by giving her what she wanted but on my terms.

When I was ready to put my plan into action, I knocked on Bintu's door and told her I would help with the bill, but because she told me so late, I would either be late on my rent or she could subtract it from my rent. Bintu's agreed to subtract it from my rent but then I had another request... I wanted the account number and the phone number of the electricity company to make the payment directly to them so that they could get it quicker. She agreed.

Once I had in possession the information I needed to do some investigative research, I made some phone calls and I got confirmation of my suspicions. The electricity company told me that Bintu had not paid in months and that she had been issued a turn-off notice which was due soon. I went downstairs to tell the couple the information I had just found out and all they could concentrate on what the fact that the lights could get turned off. What I was trying to tell them was she had our rent money but was not paying her bills. I went to

Bintu with my confirmation of payment and I wrote out a receipt for her to sign so she would not come up with some story later about me never gave her anything toward the bill—especially since I found out she was a liar. I knew at that point she couldn't be trusted.

Several weeks later, I was laying on my bed talking to my daughter and just when I was about to get off the phone, I looked up and noticed a long crack across the ceiling that I had not noticed before. When I hung up the call, I got as close as I could get to the ceiling to get a better look at it. I told myself that maybe my imagination was getting the best of me because it had been raining so much the last couple of days. I just kept having this bad feeling in my gut and just kept pacing back in forth in my room looking at that crack. Then, I could not contain my fear anymore so I opened my door and knocked on Bintu's bedroom door. I ran downstairs and knocked on their bedroom door yelling for everyone to come to my bedroom to look at the crack on my ceiling. Everyone came to my room and they were like, "What is the emergency?" I pointed to the ceiling and they were like, "There's nothing wrong. It just looks like that because of all the rain." I was like, "It's more than that." Bintu suggested that if I felt unsure, she would have someone come take a look at it tomorrow. I was like, "What about tonight?" She suggested moving my bed to the other side of the room. Everyone left, so I did what she suggested and I moved my bed over.

It was the worst sleep I had since I stayed there because every time I heard a noise, I jumped and looked up because I felt like the ceiling was going to collapse any moment. When I got up for work, I decided to pack a bag and go stay somewhere else until Bintu found somebody to come check the ceiling out because I could not rest until I was sure that the ceiling was not coming down on top of my head. After I finished my shift, I decided to sit in the food court while I figured out where I was going for the night. While I was in the food court, I got a call from the lady who was renting the room in the basement and she asked me when I was coming home. I told her I had planned on not coming home that night. She told me that I needed to come home because the ceiling had fallen down on top of some of my things.

I knew it was going to happen yet still was a little shocked, so I told her I would get a ride and be there as soon as I could. I called my girl friend Alexandria to tell her what happened and then I asked her if she could give me a ride to the house. When she showed up, I got in her car she suggested that we got to the store and get a disposable camera before we get to the house. I agreed that was a great idea. We picked up the camera and headed to the house. When we got there, I let myself in. I headed upstairs immediately to my room to view the damage but I really wasn't prepared to see what happened because it looked like a scene from a natural disaster video.

My mouth flew open after seeing the view but my main thought process was *thank God that I wasn't there when it happened.* Luckily I had already moved some of my stuff to the other side of the room. The whole ceiling had come down and even all the insulation too! The scariest part was that the area where I moved my bed to was closer to where the ceiling fan was and the fan was literally hanging by a thread. It was as if if you blew too hard, it might fall off.

I turned to my friend to get the camera and began to take pictures of everything. Bintu came by to say something but I really wasn't in the mood to hear what she had to say. She told me that they put some of my things in plastic bags and moved the rest of my stuff to the other bedroom upstairs. I walked up to the room to take a look and I was so overwhelmed by the whole mess so I was like, "Let me leave the house to go somewhere to get rest so I can make a plan of what to do next." Bintu had the nerve to act like she had a problem with my friend Alexandria being in her house because she was fussing, but I ignored that. I told Bintu that she was my friend so she was with me. As we drove away, all I could think about was that I had told everybody that the crack in the ceiling was serious but nobody wanted to believe me. Then I had such a mess to deal with.

The next day, after some needed sleep, I returned to the house so that I could get a better look at how much damage had been done to all of my stuff. I was thinking of where in the world I was going to lay my head now that the room I had been renting was no longer livable. I just kept looking around shaking my head. Bintu came around and I told her some of my things got damaged. She said to make a list so that it could be submitted to the insurance company. Then I told her, "Where am I supposed to sleep since my room is messed up?" She tried to suggest the room her brother used to stay in since my stuff was already in there but I let her know that was unacceptable. I remembered how dirty he was. Then she said maybe downstairs where they had moved my bed. I told her there was no privacy down there.

Later, Bintu came to me while I was sorting through all of my clothes and shoes to see what I could salvage to say she knew someone who could come and put up a temporary wall so that I would have some sort of privacy. I said that that would work for me. Unfortunately, this solution was short lived because one morning, I woke to an awful smell coming from somewhere near me only to discover the dog had pooped on the other side of the temporary wall and the smell seeped over to my side.

There was a vent on my side and it allowed me to hear conversations coming from downstairs where the couple stays. One night, they got into a huge argument/fight and I could clearly hear him beating her. I also heard a thud and she cried out. I had heard enough to call the police, and when the police arrived at the house I went to the door, and they asked me what was going on. I pointed to the basement they knocked on the door. While I was walking back upstairs I heard her lying up a storm that nothing happened. The next day I was in the kitchen, the lady from downstairs came in and she started talking about how some people should mind their own business. She never mentioned my name but I know that the comment was directed at me. The whole time I was thinking *I should have let him beat her butt more so maybe he could've knocked some sense in her head dumb broad.* I think that that situation was the last straw that broke the camel's back, so I thought about a plan to moving out of that toxic house faster!

I had been sharing everything that I had dealing with in the house with my co-worker and friend Alexandria. I told her that I needed to find another place to live quickly and she suggested that I could come and move in with her for a while—at least until I found another spot. I told her I didn't want to inconvenience her family but she insisted that the kids could all share one bedroom. In my mind, it was the best solution because I was desperate to get out of that house. I agreed. We planned and set a date when we would start moving my stuff out that toxic house. Bintu had the nerve to come to me asking for the next month's rent, and I told her I wasn't paying rent for this makeshift room she had put me in. I also told her I have decided that I will be moving out before I pay another cent!

She went off on me like I had beat her or something then she told me she from Africa and I wasn't going to do her like that. She said she will withhold all my mail that comes to the house. I then raised my voice over hers to tell her, "Wait a minute! You are currently in the United States where it is illegal and a federal crime to withhold someone's mail. I have every right to leave! You take my security deposit money and use that, but anything else you will not be getting from me unless you take me to court!" I slammed the door at her and entered my makeshift room.

The next day, Alexandria and I were set to move me out of the hell hole I had been staying in. Cue the music for the dramatic scene that transpired next... Alexandria called to tell me she was on the way so I began to move some of my things close to the door so I could take them straight out to the car. When Alexandria pulled up, I opened the door to let her in so she could help me with my stuff. Bintu went off on some rant which I was totally ignoring but I did take the time to reiterate to her, "I told you I was moving." When I come back inside after putting the first load in the car, I heard Bintu on her cellphone. I figured she was on the phone with the police telling them some strange woman has entered her house and how she didn't know her. She started breathing hard and made it sound like she was upset while fake crying. I couldn't believe my ears or eyes—the act this woman was portraying! I was yelling over her, saying she was lying so I shook my head while I continued packing.

When I went outside, I was telling Alexandria what I just overheard Bintu doing and the next thing we knew, we saw cops with guns drawn surrounding us. I found myself in such great fear for my life so I starting yelling with our hands in the air, "We are not harming anybody... this is a great big misunderstanding and a civil matter only... please let me explain." By the grace of God, the officer in charge gave an order to the other officers to put their guns down. I explained the whole situation to the lead officer. I told him that she only called them because she was angry at me for moving out and that she felt like I still owed her money. He said, "Well that IS a civil matter." I said, "Exactly. Can you explain that to her?"

The scariest part of the whole situation was that several weeks prior, there was a home evasion several doors down from Bintu's house. That's why the mindset of the officers probably was *it's the same people hitting another house* which could have caused the whole incident to have had a deadly consequence. All because this deceitful, lying, mean, cunning, demonic, evil, and ugly inside woman couldn't manipulate me to do what she wanted me to do to keep financing her African projects and shopping sprees.

Needless to say, we left after that last load, but I did turn and give her butt one last look saying *you messed with the wrong sista*! I did have to make several more trips back to the house to get the rest of my things that I left behind after that day, but I covered myself to have the police to explain to her that she had to let me back into the house to get the rest of my belongings so there weren't any more problems with that. At one point, I really wanted to sue her over everything that happened the whole time I was in the house, but in the end I was simply just glad to be out of there.

Chapter 10

Vagabond Blues

F inally, I had a fresh new start at a new place and everything seemed to be a great fit for me at Alexandria's house. Technically, *anything* was great after the last living situation I just left—or so I thought. Alexandria's children were great entertainment for me and they seemed to really like me since I noticed that I could get them to do things that their mother had a hard time getting them to do... I was by no means a perfect mother figure, but I also had already raised my kids mainly by myself so I had a little more experience.

Alexandria's household consisted of her, her husband, and their three young children. Before I moved in, I was made aware that there were some marital problems going on. It came as no surprise to me when some arguments would break out between them. I felt like my role in the household was to keep quiet and just comfort the children by keeping them entertained in my room so they would be distracted from what was going on with their parents.

In my opinion, things hit an all-time low when Alexandria and her husband made an agreement to have an open marriage. I guess in their minds this would cause less tension between them, and even though I had never been married before, I knew this wasn't a good idea. However, it was none of my business. Alexandria then came to tell me that they have agreed on a schedule of when they would take turns going out with other people. I was sitting there taking it all in and biting my tongue, but at the same time I knew that she just wanted me to listen—not respond. It did not take long before this plan blew up on them and turned to major turmoil in the household. One night, Alexandria decided she was going to take advantage of the fact that it was her husband's night out and she invited some guy over to the house. Her husband decided to come home early and the guy was still downstairs. Even though I was upstairs in my room with my door closed, I could hear all the commotion. I could clearly hear her tell the guy to go out the back door and her husband was banging on the front door telling her to let him in. I guess he figured out something was up and was headed to the back door apparently armed with a knife. I heard her yelling at her husband to put the knife away. The whole time I was upstairs, praying I didn't have to call 911 for the police to come. The commotion died out, and I guess the guy got away.

The next morning, she came to me to tell me about what happened last night. This time I did not hold back how I felt about what she did and how wrong she was. I said it wasn't funny at all and I asked her, "How do think your kids would have felt if your husband killed that man and went to jail all because of what you did?" I think it was the first time she stopped and thought about her actions while playing this emotional control game with her husband.

If only this was wildest thing she would do, it would have been bearable but instead of correcting her behavior, things got even crazier. When it was her night to go out, she decided to stay out all night only to return in the morning. It became a problem because they only had one car. It was weird seeing and hearing her husband call her to see if she was on the way home because he needed to go to work. He had to wait around until she got home to get the car keys. One evening, I came to the house after working late and saw all these people standing outside, not knowing that there was some sort of impromptu party going on. I walked inside the house and I noticed that Alexandria's daughter was sitting on the floor in between several intoxicated men. I picked her up and started calling for her mother. Alexandria peeked through the door and asked what was going on. I yelled at her to come get her daughter and I placed her in her arms while she looked at me like she didn't understand why I was so upset. I said, "You shouldn't be leaving your daughter in here with these men while you are outside where you cannot keep an eye on her." I proceeded to walk upstairs to my room so that I could try to have some peace and quiet while this makeshift drinking party continued throughout the night.

Not long after, my friend and her husband decided that they were not reconciling their marriage. They decided that her husband should move out of the house and it seemed like a good solution which would be an end to the arguing. But then I found out that she has befriended this young man who was just getting out of the detention center. It was bad enough she was seeing him in the first place, and then she made a decision to move him in. I felt bad when she did that because I wasn't always there to protect her children all the time.

This guy was not only young, but he was as dumb as a bag of bricks too. Alexandria had to take the boys to the doctor's one day and she didn't feel like taking her daughter along, so she decided to leave her behind. I didn't realize this until I was on my way out the door. I stopped in my tracks when I heard her daughter crying and I also heard her simple boyfriend cussing at her. I turned around to go look for some clothes for her daughter so she could come with me. I could not with good conscience leave her daughter there alone with that guy because I did not trust him and I would never forgive myself if something happened after I left her there even though she was not my child. The interesting thing was that she never asked me why I took her daughter with me, but she did not care if she did not have to watch her along with the boys.

One evening, I was upstairs with the kids and Alexandria made an effort to put the children to bed so she could have some alone time with the young boy downstairs and I said to her, "You know your son is going to get back up to look for you." She said he was sleeping so I said okay jokingly, knowing that I paid attention to her son's sleep patterns. The next thing I knew I heard her son calling her name and I hear him walking down the steps. No, I didn't stop him from walking in on them but I did hear her scream out as he walked up to them while they were in the middle of doing the wild thing.

I cannot remember the last time I laughed so hard. I said in my head *I told her that was going to happen* but she didn't believe me. It just proved that I paid attention to her children's habits more than she did. With all that happening in the house, I only felt bad about the things that directly affected the children because they did not have a choice other than be there and they were depending on their parents.

While I was in my room one day, I heard Alexandria's son cry out so loud it got me concerned so I opened my door and headed down the steps. As I was going down, the young boyfriend was coming upstairs quickly past me. As I got to the bottom of the stairs and walked over to Alexandria's son he was still crying. I got close enough to whisper, "Did he just hit you?" He nodded his head at me. I whispered back to him: "The next time you see your father, tell him what happened." Then I went into the kitchen where Alexandria was cooking and washing clothes. I walked near her to say, "How are you just letting that guy hit your child?" She looked at me laughing then said he was only playing with him. I told her, "Why would a man his age be playing with your young son? By the way, you didn't hear him crying? He just told me that the young boy hit him. Go ask your son." When we walked over to him, he confirmed what I told her, and she still acted like she did not believe her own son.

Later I had a conversation with a young lady named Lacy who would watch Alexandria's children while she was working and we became friends. I told her about the situation with the young boyfriend hitting Alexandria's eldest son. We both agreed that we were going to keep our eyes open and that if we witness any other situation regarding this boyfriend abusing any of the children, we would report it to the father and/or the authorities.

One night I came home and as I walked through the door; I was approached by Alexandria saying that someone had called her husband to tell them that her son had been abused by her boyfriend. She got all in my face, basically accusing me of being the person that made the call. All that I had been holding back came out my mouth. I said, "No way did I make the call but I was glad somebody did since you seem to be so blind as to what is happening with your children." When I looked around, I saw Lacy's face and I knew it was her who made the call, but I was not even mad at her.

Later, when things calmed and Alexandria went upstairs, I went into the kitchen so Lacy and I could have a conversation without being overheard by Alexandria. She confided in me that she made the call to Alexandria's husband after seeing bruises on Alexandria's son. I agreed that that was a good move because if she had not done it, I probably would have. I was really starting to feel extremely uncomfortable about the situation because there are some things I will put up with, but situations concerning children I will not tolerate.

I mentioned to Lacy that I needed to move out of the house before everything went from bad to worse and she offered to let me come stay with her if I needed to.

The next day, I was in my room with the door open when I heard the house phone. I could hear Alexandria raising her voice and then I heard her say, "Don't nobody know nothing about what happened because they didn't see him put his hand on my child." As I was listening in on the conversation, I detected that she was talking to her mother who must be talking about the bruises on her son. I was determined to listen to everything she said to her mother so that I could call her on her lies later. Then I heard her say, "These bitches always got some lies coming out of their mouths." That was when lost it. I waited until I heard her hang up the phone first, then I proceeded down the steps. I stopped mid-way before I looked down at her in her eyes as she looked up at me. Then I said, "So I am a bitch now!"

She looked at me startled when I asked her questions about what I had overheard her say. Then she said, "I never called you a bitch." I said, "Then who were you were referring to when you were talking to your mom just now?" I then repeated parts of her conversation that I heard where she told her mother *that nobody saw nothing, so these bitches need to mind their business and stop trying to cause problems for me.* I told her, "The only person you could have been referring to is me." At that point my anger boiled over and I began to run down everything I had witnessed since I had lived there but most importantly, the recent incidents that happened.

Then I began to run down how she was in complete denial of incidents going on in her own house. I was like, "How are you going to say nothing happened with your son when you and I talked to your son and he clearly told you that your boyfriend hit him? She said she didn't remember that, so I smirked and said, "I guess you don't remember—so now you have a convenient case of amnesia. Did you ever ask, in the beginning when I moved in why I took your daughter with me the day that you took the boys to the doctor's office? Because you never asked me why." She said, "I figured that she just asked if she could go." I said, "No. You left her here by herself with your boyfriend and he was cursing her out so I was worried that he might hurt her. That's why I took her with me."

Alexandria kept a shocked look on her face the more I revealed to her, and I was not moved so then I reminded her... "In the beginning when I moved, I would always look out for your children... I can't stand by any longer while I witness what is going on without saying anything anymore." Then I told her that I have decided to move out. I walked back upstairs to the room. I proceeded to call my son to tell him that I needed his help to move at the end of the week but he suggested we should plan for an earlier move. I had to make some calls to Lacy who had offered to let me stay with her so that I could get out of this mess that was going on at Alexandria's house. After many calls to Lacy, she agreed to let me move in earlier than we had discussed. I called my son back to let him know that I would be ready to move the next day and I let Alexandria know I was moving tomorrow.

The worst part about moving was that I feared for the children's wellbeing with Alexandria's boyfriend still living there. It was hurting me so bad that all I did was cry and pray as I packed my stuff to move. It turned out to be an overwhelming job preparing for the move and unfortunately, I was not exactly ready when my son showed up, but I did manage to get all my stuff moved in one night.

———⚬⚭⚬⚭⚬⚭⚬———

I moved in with Lacy and her young daughter while her daughter's father was in prison. Lacy and I got along well but as time went on, the living situation became a little awkward because her family lived in the same complex and her parents lived about ten minutes away in the same neighborhood as Alexandria.

A couple of weeks after I moved in, Lacy's mother called her to tell her what happened at Alexandria's house after I left. There was an instance where her argument with her boyfriend got so heated that police got involved. All I kept thinking about was thank God I had moved out when I did because I could have been all caught up in their messy shenanigans!

Lacy's family coming over was only awkward when they'd come over and smoke weed together. It was so strong at times that I would try breathing through my open windows and later when they left, there would be a cloud of smoke left behind. That kind of situation gave me migraines because I didn't even smoke regular cigarettes.

I was working at Macy's and sometimes I would work long shifts with the mindset that I was saving up my money to get a car and I would have more doors opened (career wise) to get another job paying more money to move. I overheard Lacy talking about how her daughter's father was trying to get an early release from prison and I know living in the same house would be very uncomfortable since it was already awkward when she had guys over while I was there. We always tried to give each other our space but it was a small apartment.

———ᴎᴏᴏᴇᴛᴏᴏᴛᴏᴏᴏᴎᴎ———

I had been seeing this guy on and off then one day, out the blue after he celebrated his birthday, he asked me to marry him. I was truly shocked. His reasoning was that we weren't getting any younger and we had known each other for a while. I went along with that reasoning. Then, a week later he became very distant and started calling me less so finally I questioned him about how he was acting.

He told me he got cold feet after thinking about it and I thought the explanation was strange. I said, "You were the one who brought it up to me. Now you want to pull back?" I made up my mind to give him lots of space.

Meanwhile one of my new roommate's family members came over from time to time, always having positive things to say and always complimenting my looks but I really wasn't paying him much attention. For one thing, I was practically engaged and he was much younger than me. As things fell apart with my then ex-fiancé, Derrick was now appearing to be someone to pay attention to and it was not like I had not ever dated someone younger than me before. I made comments about our age difference, but he said it didn't matter to him. The more time we spent talking to each other, the closer we became. Then it became a secret relationship and I guess the fact that we were sneaking around made it even more exciting... until he put his focus on a new girl who was much younger than me.

The worst part was he would bring the other girl to the apartment. I was so jealous, hurt, and angry because he would want me to leave the apartment on my days off so that he could spend time with the other girl.

After getting past that, I got refocused on my goal and income tax time was around the corner. I knew I had a refund coming so I was finally going to be able to get my car. When the money hit my account, I already had a plan as to how much I wanted to spend and how much I was setting aside for any additional repairs, tags, title, and inspection costs but I was lacking the skills to find the right type of car I needed.

I called up my ex-boyfriend Larry for help. Larry found me a car in my price range which I was happy about until I took it through inspection and found out what needed to be done to pass the MD state inspection. Even though I called on Larry for his help to get the repairs done and I had drained all my discretionary money set aside, I was still having problems.

Then one day, Lacy told me that the rental office had put a notice on the door talking about how they were coming around to do inspections of the apartments. That meant that I needed to put my stuff up in the bedroom because I wasn't supposed to be living with her because I am wasn't on the lease. The day our apartment was scheduled for inspection, I was running late for work. While I was on the bus, it hit me that I forgot to put my stuff up in the bedroom. When I got home that night, Lacy told me that a person from the rental office had made a comment to her about the fact that they knew that I was staying with her and that if I didn't move out within 30 days, they would evict her.

It was as if the ground sank underneath me when she told me that. I went into panic mode because I had just spent all my money on my lemon car that I could have used to move. If only I had known earlier, I would have postponed some things on the car which was having so many problems I was not even able to drive it. I did the only thing I knew that would work and that was getting down on my knees to pray so that God could reveal a solution to me. I had 30 days to come up with a solution.

There was one good thing that happened during this 30-day period though, and that was finally getting a chance for an interview with a major bank. As the days to my interview were counting down, I was getting nervous about where I would go with no real emergency funds to go to another place. I would check in with God from time to time to remind Him of my plight, of course.

One day I had a doctor's appointment and as I went to sign in I noticed there were some fliers sitting on the counter. I quickly glanced at them then nonchalantly picked one up as I waited for them to call my name. The words nearly jumped off the page at me: Homeless Resource Day. The flier went on to list all the agencies that would be represented at this program. I was excited at the prospect of having an answer to my situation. Then, I looked at the date and the time but I was scheduled to work on that day. I kept thinking *I must get to this event.* I started thinking about how I could do both on that day, so I called my job to ask if it was okay if I came later that day. They said it wouldn't be a problem.

Finally, I began to see some light at the end of the tunnel so I made a plan on how to handle that day when it arrived. I took the bus to get to the event and walked up to the school where the event was being held. When I walked inside, I was truly amazed to see how organized the event was. As soon as you stepped inside, you were greeted by an assigned person who would take you around the building to any and all the different stations that you signed up for on your initial paperwork. The woman who was assigned to me had to have been sent from heaven because she was so kind and helpful.

I had mentioned to her at the beginning that I was on a tight timeframe because I had to get to work quickly and my time was running short. She turned to me with a voice of wisdom to say, "I know you have to go to but how often do you have the opportunity to apply for all the agencies in the same place?" I agreed then I called my job to let them know that I was going to be later than I had initially said.

While at the event, I was able to put my name on several lists for housing and at a shelter as well. The days going by just had me on the edge of my seat. I had a phone number for the shelter and I began to call every other day until they started calling me back. Finally, we stopped playing phone tag with one of the head ladies and she asked me to come to the shelter because they had an opening coming up soon.

I went to the shelter and talked to one of the head counselors where she explained the rules and regulations and showed me around. We also set a date that I would be moving in. I went back to the apartment and told Lacy how I would moving out next week. She asked me where I was going so I told her I was going to the shelter because I couldn't afford anywhere else to live since I spent my money on my lemon car. I noticed how she seemed to act really funny toward me after that, but I wasn't quite sure if it was because she would miss the money I was giving her, if it was because her daughter's father was coming home earlier than she had predicted, or if it was her feeling guilty about lying to me about the real reason why she wanted me out.

Deep down I wondered if she lied about what the rental office said. It really did not matter to me and I was not mad at her either way because she let me stay for a good amount of time and she did not have to. Soon I got a phone call to come in for a second interview at the bank and I could not believe it when I realized it was for the same day I was scheduled to move into the shelter. I did not know how I was going pull it all together, but I just had to. it was a bit overwhelming trying to set everything in place.

The morning came and I went on the interview. It was only the second time that I was involved in a group interview and after listening to the other candidates talk, I knew I was finally on my way to a new career. I had to rush back to the apartment to finish packing my stuff so I could head to the shelter. I had to make a stop before catching another bus to the apartment and while I waited, I called a good friend of mine—Don Juan—to tell him I had decided to go to the shelter for a while until I got back on my feet. I told him about how good I felt about my job interview too. Don Juan asked if I needed his help and I finally admitted to myself that I did need help so I told him yes. He then asked if he could meet me at the apartment so I wouldn't have to call a cab.

I thought I had already packed most of my stuff that I was taking with me but I hadn't done enough, and the next thing I knew Don Juan was downstairs waiting on me so I had to rush. I was really tired of going up and down the stairs carrying my stuff to his car. I had to be careful because they had shown me a diagram of how little the space where I would keep all my stuff was and it was not much space at all. It was an overwhelming feeling I had when we pulled up in front of the shelter not knowing what to expect or which direction I was heading towards from there.

Chapter 11

Diamond in the Rough

James 1:2-4

"Consider it pure joy, my brothers, and sisters, whenever you face trials of many kinds, because you know that the testing of your faith produces perseverance. Let perseverance finish its work so that you may be mature and complete, not lacking anything."

For the first time in my life, I felt like I was in a place where I reached a challenge that I did not know if I could overcome. I did know mentally and spiritually that I could persevere through it and I had to keep reminding myself of the scripture Philippians 4:13: "I can do all things through Christ who strengthens me!"

It was not until I entered the shelter that I realized how much of a sheltered life I had really lived, and I must have been living in a bubble for most of my life. I had so many issues going on in my life during that time.

I arrived at the shelter and one of the first things required was to do an intake evaluation. The young lady who was assigned to do it was a warm disabled young woman who was good at getting to the root of some of my greatest issues in life. One of the questions she asked me was to list all of the tragedies that I have experienced. As I began to relive and tell her each painful revelation, I began to cry from just the horrible memories. Then, I looked up through my tears and realized that the young lady had stopped typing. She looked at me directly and said, "Wow you are a strong woman." I said, "I am?" It was at that point for the first time in my life that I thought about how much God had helped me through and how others may not have made it through what God allowed me to survive.

God was ministering to me through this young woman because I kept asking myself over and over in my mind *how did I get here?* Then she told me to look at this moment as the beginning of a new chapter in my life. For the first time, through this moment I saw a light at the end of the tunnel.

I was so ashamed of the fact that I ended up in the shelter that I only let a very select few friends know where I was. Unfortunately, due to my lack of transportation due to my lemon car, I was limited on my travels including church. I didn't realize how much spiritual covering I had while going to church until I was inside the shelter and I had a meltdown one day. It was because I had begun to carry the heaviness of some of the women who were in there and I began to cry uncontrollably for hours and I ended up having to talk to three different counselors to help me understand what was causing my emotional breakdown.

The bottom line was, I figured out later on my own—as I was writing this book, actually—that I was experiencing a moment of being an empath. I was going through so many car issues and every time I thought that I had got to the root of the problems it was always another problem, so I was being drained financially. I had to report all my expenses to my counselor and I was advised that in order to save towards my goal of having money to move out, I needed to give up my car.

Because of this I and one of the ladies I befriended at the shelter decided to take a field trip to the junkyard on one of the hottest days of the year to surrender my car.

———ᴡᴡᴏᴏᴇᴛᴏᴏᴛᴏᴏᴡᴡ———

The best avenue I had to getting fed spiritually while I was in the shelter was that we would receive dinners prepared by local churches. Then there was my youngest daughter who was having issues with her living arrangements and the thought that she could end up here was frightening. If that wasn't enough of disappointment then I found out that she was put on academic probation and she was denied housing on campus I was having a hard time concentrating on my stuff when my youngest was going through her stuff and as a mother, I couldn't turn off my emotions even though I was in the middle of my own mini crisis.

Finally, I heard that my youngest daughter will be moving in with some of her cousins. That was a big weight off my mind. I was not happy to hear from my daughter that she told her cousins that I am in the shelter, but it was already too late.

———ᴡᴡᴏᴏᴇᴛᴏᴏᴛᴏᴏᴡᴡ———

If it wasn't for my friend Christa, my stay while I was in the shelter would have been unbearable. She was a shoulder to cry on, my road dog, supporter—all the necessary qualifications for a real good friend. I had a few verbal run-ins with some of the women there mainly because I had to get up early for work while they wanted to stay up playing their music and watching movies inside the dorm areas. The others had all kinds of alarms and ringtones going off throughout the morning.

———wmooevoovoovm———

Throughout my stay in the shelter, women were coming and going so some of them were moving out to the transitional house located behind the shelter. One of the women who was stirring up stuff between me and some of the other women in the shelter got approved to move to the transitional housing, so I was incredibly happy!

The shelter was divided into three parts: the women's side, men's side, and the family floor. While we were there, this woman came in with her daughter but it did not take long to notice that something was off about their family dynamic. There were times that Christa and I would witness different situations while we were in the dining area then look at each other with the *did you just see that* look. We would find a way to be alone and have a discussion that something was off. When I was just hanging around the shelter on my days off, I started noticing the young girl being around several people who weren't her mother. She was even left unsupervised which was against the rules of the shelter but what sent my friend and me over the edge was seeing the little girl's interaction with some of the men but no reactions from her mother to correct her.

We took it upon ourselves to go to the higher ups to voice our concerns and in my mind what it looked like was this young girl had been exposed to some very grown up things or been involved in some child molestation situations.

———wmooevoovoovm———

There were many nights I didn't get much sleep. At first it was because I was fearful of my surroundings. Then it was because I had a woman who slept across from me who was under the influence of some heavy medications. She would wake up in the middle of the night and literally lean so far over that she would almost fall off her bed. I would wake her up and tell her to lay down in her bed then in the morning she would thank me.

In one of the meetings with my counselor, she presented me with an invitation to move to the Willow House (the transitional house) and I immediately turned down the offer because all I could think about was that old mean crow living over there.

I had started seeing this bus driver for a while and it was great having someone paying attention to me and taking me away from the shelter but he had some baggage with this woman living in his home that he claimed he had no attachment to but she wouldn't leave his house and he wasn't about to leave either. I would try to put her out of my mind but that elephant would come up every time we went out because we couldn't go certain places in case we would run into people who knew them then one day we had made plans to go places then she called and he stopped everything to go to her side. I had enough of the nonsense, so I told him I was ready to go our separate ways then I started concentrating on my new career.

I had been hired by the major bank and what came next was figuring out how to get to the training which was near Baltimore. I no longer have my own transportation so I petitioned to the shelter for help. They gave me money and directions on how to get to the training. The first day of travel was a disaster and my commute was extremely long. It seemed as if I was leaving in the dark and coming back in the dark. I happened to tell one of the guys in the shelter about my long travel to and from training so he offered to take me or bring me back which was a blessing. It had been my desire for so long to change my career and I was finally on my way, but as it goes, *be careful what you ask for because you just might get it.*

Meanwhile during my weekly meeting with my counselor, she asked me again if I was ready to move into the Willow House and again, I told her no because the troublemaker was still living in the house. After some time, I finished my training with the bank, and it was time for some actual on the job training at a branch within walking distance from the shelter. That was great after having to take 3 buses to get to training.

While I was looking forward to starting work at the bank, I never took into context the fact that I was going to be the only person of color working there. In my excitement, it never crossed my mind that it would become an issue at all. Several days after starting work at the branch, I was leaving the lobby area heading to the teller line when I opened the door to see the tellers and the branch managers standing there. Then I heard the branch manager say the F-bomb. I just stood there in shock and I saw the look of embarrassment on the tellers' faces when they saw my face.

A week later I met with my counselor and again she asked me if I was ready to move into the Willow House after I had complained of issues inside the dorms. This time I didn't say no as quickly. Then she said, "Well isn't better to deal with only four other women as opposed to fourteen other women?" When she put it like that I said, "You're absolutely right I'm ready to go!" The sad part about that time was that my friend Christa had got approved for an apartment and I felt like I was left to the wolves without protection but I was happy for her because she really needed her own place.

The next uncomfortable situation during that time of my life was at work. I was telling my co-workers about an incident that happened at the shelter and the branch manager was standing on the other side when she blurted out "Oh, is that why you ended up in the shelter—because of drugs and alcohol? I was in such a shock when she said that that I just froze.

I looked around to see how many people heard her say that to me and the look on my co-worker's face said it all. I told her that wasn't the reason and it was because of an economic situation, but from that day forward I regretted that I had shared with them that I was homeless. I initially did so thinking she would give me more hours so that I could save money faster to move out on my own.

Several months later, I received a move-in date to the Willow House but I was still a little nervous about the eventual showdown I was going to have with the she-devil that was still in there. I prayed that God would give me the strength to deal with her. Another woman came into the shelter and we quickly became friends and I thanked God for her because at one point I mysteriously got ill and when I went to the urgent care center they couldn't find anything. They sent me back to the shelter with some pain medicine but my new friend told me that I was moaning in pain all night. I ended up going to the emergency room at Anne Arundel hospital where after some tests they saw a cyst and recommended I go to a specialist.

I had to call out of work for a couple of days and I wasn't able to get an appointment with a specialist until I returned to work which made my supervisors mad, but I had to do what was best for me. They made me feel really uncomfortable when I returned because they kept questioning me about medications I was on, my diagnosis, did I really need to go to my doctor's appointment... just very negative comments and I was so upset that I told my counselor about the things that they questioned me about. She told me that their line of questioning was against the HIPPA laws which I did not know about.

After that talk with my counselor, I had more knowledge about my rights and I was ready for them when I went back to work just in case they tried to come at me wrong again. When I went to the doctor's appointment, the doctor was not able to determine what caused my severe pain. She said the cyst should have not caused the pain I suffered and there was no way to determine if the pain would return.

———— ∿⦿⧀⦿⧁⦿⧂∿ ————

Eventually my move date would come, and it was difficult to move and not be able to take time off but even though I was exhausted it still felt good. As I sat in my room with a locked door and total silence since my tv hadn't arrived yet, I can still remember how frustrated I had become at the shelter and how all I wanted to do was have peace and quiet. It was so funny how I just wanted to get some rest and when I could finally rest, I stayed up late.

When I moved in to the Willow House, I had to pay rent and buy groceries too which I had not even thought about for a long time. I put my stuff in storage, but I did not even have any dishes, pots and pans, or silverware. I would still go over to the shelter to eat meals since I was now responsible for buying my own food and the Department of Social Services had cut the amount of my food stamps.

On one of the occasions of going over to the shelter to eat dinner, I was looking around the room to find some of my friends that I liked to sit with. I noticed this guy staring me down sitting at the table with some other guys I knew. I sat down by a guy friend in the shelter and the whole time this guy was quiet but making me a little nervous because he was staring at me so hard. I was like *did I remind him of somebody or what?* The next night I went over to the shelter for dinner, I saw that guy again and after we finished eating dinner he came up to me and asked if he could talk to me outside. I agreed.

When we went outside, he introduced himself as Kevin, started telling me about himself and things he had been through then he asked me if he could have my phone number. He was truly rough around the edges. I did give him my number and we started talking and hanging out together. One of the biggest rules at the Willow House is no men allowed upstairs and many times we broke the rules. One night, we got caught by the troll who stayed downstairs in the house which was bad news for me because the last thing I needed was for her to have something on me that she could use against me and I just gave her some ammunition.

She got back at me but not in the way that I thought cause she started making our lives miserable in little annoying ways. When we would be in the living room watching movies she would come out her room talking about the volume was too loud or she would talk real loud on her phone while in her room knowing that we were in the living room trying to have some private time away from the shelter. There were only four women to deal with in the Willow House but no loss on the drama but sometimes I felt like I was the only sane and competent woman in the house.

One night I was trying to go to bed because I had to work the next day but several of the ladies were talking in the hall near me and they were pretty loud. I opened up my door and asked them to please lower their voices so that I could get to sleep, then I closed my door. The next morning I was on my way out for work and as I was passing through the kitchen, I noticed a book on the counter that was about angels. I noticed that there was a knife stabbed through the middle of the book and for some reason, I immediately knew someone was sending me a message but I just continued to head out to work.

When I returned to the house later I got confirmation from one of the other ladies that what I saw left on the counter was definitely a message left for me because the cat lady as I call her got mad that I asked her to be quiet and she went off after I closed the door. I had taken a picture of what I saw and since I took it as a threat, I decided that I should show it to someone at the shelter in the morning before going to work. I showed it to the head guy who said he would do something about it. In the meantime, the cat lady was acting up every time she saw me saying all kinds of mean stuff and cussing at me. I went back over to the shelter to see what they planned to do to her since she was harassing me.

Over at work, one of my co-workers resigned to take a job elsewhere which left a full-time position open. I wanted to apply for the position but I heard the hesitation in my manager's voice. I couldn't understand since I was already doing the job just on a part-time basis. I was even getting there earlier than some of co-workers and I was taking the bus or getting rides so I deserved that position even though she acted like she didn't want me to have it. She couldn't justify not giving it to me, so she did.

I was proud at first for stepping into the full-time position but then another teller was leaving, and I had so much extra duties put on me and it became overwhelmingly stressful. During that time, I didn't realize that I was getting close to my one-year mark at the Willow House which meant that I would be eligible to get a Section-8 voucher to move out with.

While Kevin and I had become close, the old bus driver tried to come back around but I told him I was with someone else now. Kevin got jealous so out of nowhere, he proposed to me and presented me with a ring. I accepted even though in my heart I felt like he did it to make sure the other guy would stop coming around. We had a discussion about how we should try to get an apartment on our own because I had a good job and he was working two jobs. We started applying for apartments but one of the charges he had on his record causes us to be denied each time we tried to get an apartment. We even went to our pastor to see if someone they had a connection with could help us get into an apartment. Even with all that help it still didn't work. He even petitioned the judge to shield the charge but the judge denied his request each time.

We had to accept the fact that the only way to get a place would be for me to go ahead and apply for the voucher. I was feeling so anxious between dealing with the whole voucher process and the pressure from Kevin. He was on borrowed time because the Director at the shelter and his counselor let him know that his time there was coming to an end and he needed to make some plans real soon as to where he was going. He kept buying time by telling them he was leaving with me, but my stuff was being held up due to the long process of the paperwork.

When the paperwork was finally processed the next phase was to pick a place to move to that would accept the voucher which turned out to be another adventure. I then had to deal with the apartment complex which was a big wait-and-see step. The next thing I had to figure out was what I was going to do about my job situation because without a car, I wasn't going to be able to commute to my job.

I discovered that my company had another branch located near where I was planning to move to and I found out there was a full-time teller position open. I found out that the company didn't do transfers so I had to apply as a first-time candidate. Everybody including myself knew without a doubt though that I was in because they didn't need to train me at all. I did the interview with that branch manager and just waited for word from the recruiter. Several days later I got a call from the recruiter... but was not at all what I expected. She told me the branch manager decided to hire someone else. I wasn't the only one shocked. Everyone at my branch was surprised.

I had a little talk with God to say *how are you going to open the door for me to move into my own place and I don't have a job...* I was truly confused about the direction He was taking me. I had to put in my resignation and on top of that, there was complete silence regarding the move-in date at the complex and it seemed like they were giving me the run-around. I was getting really nervous so I made friends with one of the ladies in the rental office. I even broke down in tears while telling her my story of thanking God for bringing me out of the grips of the shelter to coming out and getting my own apartment. When I got in touch with her to find out why I hadn't heard anything about my move-in date, she instructed me on what to do.

I knew I was on work time but I had to take some drastic measures because I didn't come that far just to back down, so I wrote a long email to the head Resident Manager of the complex and explained that I had submitted everything that they had asked for. I ran down a timeline then closed with "So I am wondering why I haven't received any word from you as to when I will be moving in." It worked. He made sure I received an exact confirmation of a move-in date and the joy I felt preparing for the move and leaving my job was so great because it was only possible because I stood solid on my faith in God that He would bring me out!

When I look back, I realize that God was taking me through the diamond making process because in order come out as a true diamond, we have to be put under pressure, extreme heat, and then cut into the diamonds that we are destined to be!

STILL I RISE

BY MAYA ANGELOU

You may write me down in history
With your bitter, twisted lies,
You may trod me in the very dirt
But still, like dust, I'll rise.

Does my sassiness upset you?
Why are you beset with gloom?
'Cause I walk like I've got oil wells
Pumping in my living room.

Just like moons and like suns,
With the certainty of tides,
Just like hopes springing high,
Still I rise

Did you want to see me broken?
Bowed head and lowered eyes?
Shoulders falling down like teardrops,
Weakened by my soulful cries?

Does my haughtiness offend you?
Don't you take it awful hard
'Cause I laugh like I've got gold mines
Diggin' in my own backyard

You may shoot me with your words,
You may cut me with your eyes,
You may kill me with your hatefulness,
But still, like air, I'll rise.

Does my sexiness upset you?
Does it come as a surprise
That I dance like I've got diamonds
At the meeting of my thighs

Out of the huts of history's shame
I rise
Up from a past that's rooted in pain
I rise
I'm a black ocean, leaping and wide,
Welling and swelling I bear in the tide.

Leaving behind nights of terror and fear
I rise
Into a daybreak that's wondrously clear
I rise
Bringing the gifts that my ancestors gave,
I am the dream and the hope of the slave.
I rise
I rise
I rise.

Closing Note From The Author

In retrospect, because of all of my trials and tribulations that I endured in my life, I learned that I was stronger than I would have ever imagined due to the strength that God had equipped me with. When I escaped out of my abusive relationship, I learned about a variety of resources available to victims/survivors and the court process which led to a desire in me to be an advocate for women dealing with domestic violence issues. I did some research about sexual abuse and I began to understand many of my bad relationship choices and I was finally able to see why I never felt like I deserved to be with a man who loves me and cherishes me for the queen that I am. Today, I can smile every time I see her in the mirror!